Deacons and the Church

Deacons and the Church

Making connections between old and new

John N. Collins

GRACEWING

MOREHOUSE PUBLISHING
HARRISBURG, PENNSYLVANIA

First published in 2002
jointly

in England by   and in the United States of America by

Gracewing   Morehouse Publishing
2 Southern Avenue   4775 Inglestown Road
Leomister   Harrisburg
Herefordshire HR6 0QF Pennsylvania 17112

Library of Congress Cataloging-in-Publication Data

Collins, John N. (John Neil), 1931-
  Deacons and the church: making connections between old and new/John N. Collins.
    p. cm.
  Includes bibliographical references and index.
  ISBN 0-8192-1933-9
  1. Deacons--History.   I. Title.

BV680.C62 2003
262'.14--dc21
                   2002070296

UK ISBN 0 85244 554 7
US ISBN 0 8192 1933 9

Typeset by Action Publishing Technology Ltd,
Gloucester GL1 5SR

Printed in England by MPG Books Ltd,
Bodmin PL31 1EG

Contents

Preface

This book was written for deacons of any denomination, although I hope that it may contain matters of interest also to readers who are not deacons. It does in fact raise issues of a more general nature about the church, its ministry and about our uses of the scriptures. Conceived as a book of partly instructional, partly devotional reflections on passages of the scriptures familiar to deacons, it ended up as something of an argument. Those who detect the argument and do not agree with it may yet find some points to their liking in exegetical matters.

The book would not have developed in the way it has were it not for the stimulation of writing it in Sweden, which continues to reflect so much on the place of deacons in the church. For the opportunity to devote myself to writing there I owe a great debt to Ninni Smedberg of Church House, Uppsala, for making the visit possible and for the many arrangements which made it so enjoyable and yet facilitated a tolerable level of work. I also thank Professor Sven-Erik Brodd, Dean of the Faculty of Theology in the University of Uppsala, for similar support, for warm hospitality, and for the use of facilities within the faculty. To my temporary colleague there, Sussan Olsson, my thanks for her tolerance of numerous interruptions and for various kindnesses. And to Ed

Paulette of technical support my thanks for his assistance in getting an alien notebook into the network. For use of the notebook I am grateful to my employer in Australia, Dr Anne Hunt, Principal of Loreto Mandeville Hall, Melbourne.

JNC
Samariterhemmet
Uppsala

A note about women, the church, and this book

Roman Catholic women and women of other churches who feel that authorities in their churches discriminate against them on the basis of gender in matters of ministry may come to this book looking for support in their struggle to achieve gender equality in ministerial appointments. They will find, however, that the book does not address the issue directly except in so far as women occasionally occur in the sources. The book needed to do no more than that, however, because the ancient Christian language of ministry, namely *diakonia*, is inclusive. Accordingly, every implication for ministry today that arises from the considerations presented in the following pages is equally applicable to men and women.

1

The Diakonia of Modern Deacons

The first thing we hear about deacons in today's churches is that they are servants. Servants of Christ, servants of the church, servants of the people whose gathering makes up the church, servants in the margins of the world. Books about deacons attempt to be more precise about this.

The second thing we hear is that church authorities are increasingly recognizing deacons. Until 1964 churches that followed the Roman Catholic system of a threefold ministry of bishop, priests and deacons used to ordain deacons as a first step to ordination to priesthood. In that year, however, the Second Vatican Council proposed that the order of deacons need no longer be just an introductory phase but could become a permanent ranking within the clergy. Thus what were called permanent deacons began to become a feature of churches in some regions. Today some 30,000 deacons operate in the Roman Catholic Church. Anglican churches have also adopted that system.

Many other churches, however, stem from traditions which, at the time of the sixteenth-century Reformation, had rejected the idea of deacons. They had made this decision on the grounds that the medieval deacons they knew had nothing of specific value to offer the church. In the nineteenth century, however, new types of non-ordained deacons began to emerge in Lutheran communities in

Germany. They adopted the specific responsibility of extending Christian love and service to the destitute and disabled. Their ideas and organizations quickly spread into other regions and among other traditions. And in recent times among several of these churches official recognition of deacons by way of ordination has emerged. Sometimes this recognition has extended to including deacons among members of the clergy, thus marking a return to the historic threefold ministry. Like their counterparts in the Catholic traditions, these new Protestant deacons are performing an increasing range of liturgical and public roles. Their original strong sense of being called to service in obedience to the gospel has at last prompted their churches to present them as the church's official presence in the world. Above all, the new deacons seek to be in the church the kind of deacons who functioned in its first few centuries but who were lost to it for over a thousand years largely as a result of the church's unworthy ways.

The ultimate question

In addition to hearing about deacons as ordained servants, a third thing we might hear, depending largely on the kind of church environment we live in or the kind of theological literature we read, is that some people ask awkward questions about deacons, even the ultimate question: does the church need them? Some bishops and synods actually make decisions not to allow deacons in their churches as a result of ambiguities about the identity and role of deacons. These ambiguities and the increasingly various attempts to address them are the occasion of this book. This book proposes that misunderstandings abound concerning the identity and role of the deacons in the early churches, and that it is these which contribute to the widespread unease about a renewed order of deacons at the very time when in so many areas deacons appear to be flourishing. If we can come to a clearer understanding of early deacons we ought to be in a better position to decide what we ought to aim for in deacons for churches of our times. The search for a clearer understanding is not a search for an ancient model to which today's deacons would be expected to conform. Rather, the object of the search would be to clear away misunderstandings of the early deacons so that we would be able to avoid working from unreliable models.

A broken story

As all discover when they begin to look into the question of deacons, their story has been a broken one. On the one hand a long tradition presents us with familiar icons of ancient deacons in Stephen of the Acts of the Apostles and Lawrence of third-century Rome. On the other hand, the story of deacons in those early times is obscure. The disturbing thing is that as the deacon enters history the story is almost as much about putting legal restraints on deacons as about any honourable role they may have had within communities. And eventually they almost disappear.

Across the medieval and later centuries of the western church congregations were vaguely aware of deacons as vestmented figures making cameo appearances in the high liturgies of important festivals of the church's year. In fact, for a thousand years or more these individuals were almost invariably priests disguised as deacons. Deacons reported in history were rare individuals like the scholarly Alcuin or the saintly Francis of Assisi.

The Alcuins and Francises, however, were exceptions proving the rule that 'once a deacon' the deacon always advanced from his lowly rank among the clergy to the higher rank of priesthood. So predictable was this in the Roman Catholic practice that when the Second Vatican Council of the 1960s proposed restoring the diaconate a twofold diaconate emerged. For decades the new members of the order were designated permanent deacons, with the result that deacons who are ordained as a prelude to ordination as priests came to be known as transitional deacons. Not surprisingly, in some quarters today there is a vigorous campaign to eliminate diaconal ordination as a prerequisite for ordination to the priesthood.

Catholic traditions

Changes in the Roman Catholic diaconate over the last third of the twentieth century had close repercussions in especially the Anglican communion. Both churches had of course inherited deacons from the period prior to the Reformation. Unless novel developments had occurred outside the traditional diaconate, however, it is highly unlikely that these ancient churches would have interfered with the order of their threefold ministry of bishop, priest, and deacon. This was a time-honoured ministerial order indeed, but one which had every appearance of being a comfortable ecclesiastical arrangement.

The very curious thing about maintaining the threefold order in this way was that it increasingly appeared as an expression of the churches' homage to an inherited ministry whose theological principles were obviously no longer fully understood. Far from being embarrassed at such a development, the older churches sought rather to champion what they had inherited in the face of those other new churches which had discarded the diaconate as a ministerial superfluity and made do with a twofold or even with a single order.

The situation throws some light on the more mystifying ways of theology. For a theologian within the Catholic system to ask questions about the threefold order was to live dangerously. He could find himself ejected from the clerical order – the theologian was always a priest, if he had not already become a bishop – or – but this was rare until the second half of the twentieth century – he could feel obliged to withdraw his own ministerial services. A theologian's responsibility was to protect the sacred *status quo*. The outcome, accordingly, was that these churches maintained a threefold order by the artifice of ordaining theological students as deacons while they were waiting to finish the course of studies which would qualify them for ordination as priests at the young age of about 25.

Protestant initiatives

The novel development from outside the Roman and Anglican experience which changed all this was the initiative taken by some German Lutherans in the middle of the nineteenth century. This was to introduce deacons into a church which at that time had none. The interests of these innovators were not theological, although their activities introduced a discomforting element into the modern theology of ministry.

The nineteenth-century Lutherans were not proposing to reform their theology of ministry, which was as rigid in its way as that of the Romans and the Anglicans. The initiative was, rather, entirely pastoral. Pastor Theodor Fliedner and his wife Friederike were driven by a vision to provide a Christian response to the increasing numbers of 'forsaken sick, neglected children, disheartened poor and wayward prisoners' spawned by the same socio-economic conditions which were inspiring the drafting of the Communist Manifesto. Drawing inspiration from the story in the Acts of the Apostles of how the first church responded to neglected widows by commissioning seven men, among whom was Stephen, to minister to neglected women, the Fliedners and others established the renowned Motherhouses of deaconesses for the purpose of providing services to those in need. Parallel initiatives inspired men also to take part in providing such services.

These institutions spread widely in central and northern Europe, entered North America, and were more lightly represented elsewhere. In their homelands their work expanded during the twentieth century well beyond institutions like the Motherhouses to become enmeshed in the fabric of both church and society. Their existence in the heart of German churches and their prominent place in the public life of several nations gradually made an impact on the theology of ministry on a scale which, on purely theological grounds, theologians across the centuries had not thought it proper to attempt. The reason why the emergence of a new diaconate impacted on the general theology of ministry lies in the Fliedners' understanding of the ancient title of the deacon, which in turn is tied to the traditional understanding of the story of the Seven in Acts 6.

The title of deacon

The title of deacon comes from the word *diakonos* in the Greek New Testament. Throughout history this Greek word filtered into the languages of the Christian churches as the title of the third member of the threefold ministry of bishop, priest and deacon. The process began when the Latin bible represented the Greek word with the Latin transliteration *diaconus,* and evidence of the process continuing in later European languages is recognizable in words from modern languages like *Diakon, diacono, diacre, deacon,* and so on. Clearly, the Greek word was preserved in these ways for the set purpose of designating that member of the ordained clergy who was known in the early churches by the title *diakonos.* An effective sign that this title was being treated with a special reserve and respect is that all other uses of the Greek *diakon-* words in the New Testament have always been translated by other words like *ministry* or *service.* The word *deacon* was clearly a special case. In the instance of the German deaconesses, however, while the title of deacon was retained, the church showed no interest in offering the women ordination – or those men who carried out a parallel role. For 150 years these dedicated people remained marginal to the official ministry of their church at the same time as they spent their lives performing works which they called *diakonia.*

Diakonia is the word that occurs in the story of Acts 6. In fact it occurs there twice, and these days is usually translated in the first instance as 'the distribution' of food (Acts 6:1) and in the second as 'the ministry' of the word (6:4).

Because this assumed connection between *diakonia* and food was further linked with the long tradition that identified the Seven as deacons, the nineteenth-century innovators trained women and men to be deacons in the sense of servants of those in need. This connection of the word with the notion of helping led to the formation of the German word *Diakonie*. As the social work of the deaconesses spread, the word *Diakonie* also became known across German lands as the church's form of social service. Similar neologisms appeared in neighbouring languages like those in Nordic regions and in Holland.

A ministry of service

By the middle of the twentieth century this emphasis on understanding *diakonia* as service to the needy quickly began to have an impact on how ministry generally was understood in the church. In fact theologians began to re-evaluate the fundamental nature of what was commonly called the ordained ministry. That this should happen was inevitable because in the New Testament other roles in ministry were also designated by the Greek word *diakonia*.

The developments that took place in the broader theology of ministry as a result of understanding *diakonia* as service have been featured in many books. The point here is that an attempt to recreate the office of deacon in the German Lutheran church on the basis of a nineteenth-century understanding of what *diakonia* meant in the New Testament has determined the kind of diaconal movement which had developed across the churches by the turn of the twenty-first century. This is the outside event which eventually shifted the building blocks of ministerial theology. Until this shift occurred in the 1960s churches had every intention of advancing into the new age bearing as an appendage to their theology of ordained ministry the deadweight of a moribund diaconate.

The leading edge of the new ministerial model was service. Society's need for service had been the call to which the Fliedners and their contemporaries had responded. Generations of deaconesses cultivated a spirituality based on service. Associated with their lives of service was an expanding body of theological investigations into the precise character of Christian service. Almost necessarily, spiritual advisers of the deaconesses and some interested theologians pursued these investigations along paths suggested by the very name of deacon, that is, through the ancient Greek *diakon-* words. Initial perceptions of the values carried by these terms were expounded by chaplains in addresses to deaconesses and were soon taken up by academic theologians. Uniformly they wrote of *diakonia* as a term adopted by early Christians to express the specific kind of selfless, caring, and loving service that characterized Jesus in his dealings with the lame and rejected men and women who people the gospel narratives.

Academic support for a theology of service

The first substantial academic exposition on these lines was by Wilhelm Brandt, a New Testament scholar and chaplain to deaconesses. In *Dienst und Dienen im Neuen Testament* (Service and Serving in the New Testament, 1931) he insisted that the word *diakonia* expressed a specifically Christian type of service. Brandt's linguistic assessment received full academic recognition when H. W. Beyer incorporated it into the landmark publication *The Theological Dictionary of the New Testament*. This occurred in the German edition of 1935 and thirty years later in the enormously influential English translation. From this point onwards service applied as the category within which the theology of ministry was to be constructed.

The great influences in forming a public perception that service was the original character of Christian ministry and should remain so were Eduard Schweizer in *Church Order in the New Testament* (German 1957, English 1961) and Hans Küng in *The Church* (German 1967, English 1967). Thomas O'Meara's widely read *Theology of Ministry* of 1983 (second revised edition 1999) is a striking example of how the new service-theology of *diakonia* permeates and transforms a more traditional theology of orders.

The priority given to the ideal of service in the theology of the diaconate continues to this day as an obvious trait in a wide range of books, journals, newsletters and websites. The deacon movement is rich in newsletters and websites where deacons and their directors are constantly stretching the borders of fields of service and reporting on the experiences of deacons on the margins of church or society. An ideal of service is the mainspring of what is probably the most widely read study of the diaconate, James Monroe Barnett's *The Diaconate: A Full and Equal Order* (1979, revised edition 1995). The argument is that the diaconate died its first death precisely when its focus on service was lost in the bright allure of hierarchical systems of the fourth century. Barnett wrote within the North American Anglican tradition, and his perspective of service is to be seen also in other influential publications within the Anglican tradition such as the report to the House of Bishops of the General Synod in England, *Deacons in the Ministry of the Church* (1988) and the collection of papers edited by Christine Hall, *The Deacon's Ministry* (1991).

Lutheran and Reformed diaconates

Within the Lutheran and Reformed churches of Germany and their associated churches, especially those in Nordic countries and the United States, the foundational principle of diaconate has long been service. The spirit of service is encapsulated in the German word *Diakonie,* a word formulated for the specific purpose of designating a particular style of lowly and loving Christian service. The University of Heidelberg includes an institute devoted to the scientific analysis of *Diakonie.* Its most recent major publication of over 400 pages (1990, reprinted 1994 and 1998) provides academic studies by 19 scholars of what are called biblical foundations of and perspectives on *Diakonie.* Edited by Gerhard K. Schäfer and Theodor Strohm under the

German title *Diakonie – biblische Grundlagen und Orientierungen* (Diakonia – Biblical Principles and Perspectives),
these studies exemplify a long scholarly German Lutheran
tradition of promoting service as the key to understanding
the nature and practice of diaconate.

Within the Reformed tradition, Marc Edouard Kohler
elaborated on expressions of the same value across
history and in contemporary forms of diaconate in what
was originally a Swiss work in German, *Kirche als Diakonie*
(Church as Diakonia, 1991). This soon appeared in a form
adapted to French and ecumenical experience of the
diaconate under the title *Vocation, service compris! La
diaconie de l'Église* (Vocation, Service included! The
Church's Diakonia, 1995). About the same time and from
a similar Swiss provenance appeared a celebration of
diakonia as love by Gottfried Hammann, *L'amour retrouvé*
(Love rediscovered), a survey of the ministry of the
deacon from early Christian times to those of the Protestant reform. Within the Reformed tradition the influence
of Calvin's original perceptions and arrangements for
deacons as servant members of the church has been
enormous and long lasting. Elsie Anne McKee has shown
the profound impact on his thinking of his reading of Acts
6 (*John Calvin on the Diaconate and Liturgical Almsgiving*,
1984; see also her *Diakonia in the Classical Reformed
Tradition and Today*, 1989).

Roman Catholic Permanent Diaconate

Such orientation of the modern diaconate towards works
of love and service has also characterized the development
since the Second Vatican Council of the permanent
diaconate within the Roman Catholic Church. The Council
identified three roles for this diaconate. They were 'the
ministry of the word, of the liturgy, and of charity'
(*Dogmatic Constitution on the Church*, 29). The last of these,
however, is what receives most emphasis in teachings, in
scholarly commentaries, and in pastoral training. Indeed,
it is this which also ranks highest in the aspirations of

deacons themselves, as one observes in contributions by deacons to publications like the monthly *Deacon Digest* of the United States, a country which contains the largest national body of Roman Catholic deacons in the church today – over 13,000.

The same focus appears in the more academic journal *Diaconia Christi*. This is published by the influential International Centre for the Diaconate based in Rottenburg on the Neckar, Germany. Although in the Roman Catholic tradition the term 'charity' is often preferred to the term 'service', both terms are constantly sourced to the same Greek word *diakonia* on which the German Lutheran tradition rests. A striking illustration of the persistence of this tradition appears in Rolf Busemann's study 'Der Diakon in der frühen Kirche: Neues Testament und Kirchenväter' (The Deacon in the early Church: New Testament and Church Fathers). This study appeared in the journal's last issue of the twentieth century, and it invited Roman Catholic deacons – at least those of the German tradition – to enter the new millennium on a platform of service constructed on the classic lines of the 1960s.

Other significant publications illustrate the emphasis on service in Roman Catholic thinking on diaconate. One of these is the collection of papers presented to a Belgian conference on the diaconate at Louvain-la-Neuve and published in 1997 under the title *Diaconat xxie siècle* (Diaconate for the twenty-first century). Here the prominent French theologian Hervé Legrand insisted on the primacy of charity or service in the thinking of the Second Vatican Council. In the United States in 1997 Theodore W. Kraus published *The Order of Deacons: A Second Look* for the purpose of reminding deacons of the priority of their call to service. The significance of this author's emphasis is apparent from the position that he then held as Project Director for the revision of the National Guidelines on the Diaconate in the United States. A third significant illustration is the keynote address in 1997 to the International Conference on the Diaconate at Bressanone, Italy, by the respected theologian Walter Kasper, then bishop of Rottenburg-Stuttgart and subsequently Cardinal Prefect of the Pontifical Council for Christian Unity. (His paper is published in *Diaconia Christi* 3/4 1997; see different English translations in *Deacon Digest*, March/April 1998 and at http://www.deacons.net/Articles/Kasper_1997.htm) Kasper's address takes on greater significance in the light of his role at the time as patron of the international diaconal movement; he provided a home and institutional support to the International Centre for the Diaconate after the closure of its offices in Freiburg im Breisgau. In each of these publications the role of service is constitutive of both the theology and pastoral practice of diaconate.

Questioning emerges

While this emphasis remains dominant, over recent years some questioning has emerged as to the wisdom of focusing so strongly on service as the foundational element of the diaconate. One of the recurring problems theologians have faced in attempting to develop a distinctive theology for the diaconate has in fact arisen from this foundational element of service. The problem is as simple as it is stark. If service is the defining characteristic of deacons, in what way does their involvement in works of service distinguish them from any other member of a Christian community, all of whom are called by the gospel to attend to the needs of those around them? And why are deacons commissioned to such service by the solemn ritual of ordination? Ordination makes them part of the clergy, but do they need to belong to the order of the clergy in order to feed the hungry or visit the sick?

So strongly did such questions resound in the minds of an Anglican committee in England some 30 years ago that in their report *Deacons in the Church* (1974) the committee recommended the abolition of the diaconate. This was on the grounds that its continuance would obscure the responsibility of the ordinary Christian to care for and serve those in need. While that recommendation was not taken up – indeed, as we shall shortly see, recent years have seen a strong endorsement of the diaconate within the Anglican communion both as a function within its own ordained ministry and as a ministry it can share ecumenically – questions continue to be asked about the adequacy of service as the defining characteristic of the deacon.

Diakonia reinterpreted

At the source of this disquiet lie the results of the extensive enquiry which I made in the 1970s into the meaning of the word for deacon in the early Greek-speaking church. The enquiry examined the word *diakonos* and other *diakon-* words against the background of Greek literary activity across 800 years of the classical and Hellenistic eras, and its results were published in 1990 in my book *Diakonia: Reinterpreting the Ancient Sources*. These linguistic and semantic investigations are recognized as having established that when ancient Greeks used these words they were never trying to express a notion of loving and caring service. This evaluation applies equally to the authors of the New Testament and other early Christian documents. The book summed up this aspect of the linguistic study in the words (p. 254), 'Care, concern, and love – those elements of meaning introduced into the interpretation of this word and its cognates by Wilhelm Brandt – are just not part of their field of meaning.'

In 2000 Frederick Danker brought out a third English-language edition of the classic German work by Walter Bauer, *A Greek-English Lexicon of the New Testament and other Early Christian Literature*. This third edition (known as BDAG after Bauer and the three editors involved at different times in the English-language editions, Danker, Arndt and Gingrich) was based on the sixth German edition of 1988, but the entries on the *diakon-* words virtually abandon the lexical descriptions of this sixth German edition and replace them with those provided in the research volume *Diakonia* of 1990. In addition Danker has supported the new orientation of the entries with illustrative literary samples taken from the newer research, to such an extent in fact that the entries in the third edition are twice as long as those in previous editions. This is significant scholarly endorsement of the linguistic re-interpretation of *diakonia*.

We can immediately sense that the outcome of such recent linguistic research must affect how we evaluate today a diaconate that developed since the nineteenth century on the basis that its ancient name designated it as an agency for loving service. Evaluating the service model of diaconal ministry in the light of the research, Avril Keely considered it to have suffered 'a severe, if not fatal, blow'. From an academic viewpoint, the New Testament scholar Jerome Murphy-O'Connor felt obliged to write that the book 'has forced us to rethink one of the dogmas of New Testament scholarship' (*Revue biblique* 1995). The claim of the book that *diakonia* has no reference to works of love was, however, not unprecedented. The German scholar Dieter Georgi had previously made a statement to this effect in his work on *The Opponents of Paul in Second Corinthians* (1986, German 1964), but my research volume of 1990 provided the linguistic evidence and the semantic analysis which make the new lexical description necessary. The evidence is of a kind that overturns the assumption running throughout the twentieth century that early Christians developed a special usage based on these words for the purpose of expressing a particular Christian value of service. In fact Christian usage cannot be differentiated at any point from usage in Greek literature generally. A seeming exception to this assessment is the fact that the word *diakonos* did become a title of the Christian deacon in a situation otherwise unknown in Greek culture, but even here the semantic value of the word as assistant or personal attendant of another member of the community is not new.

Theologians react

In the claim that *diakon-* words must be removed from the semantic field of caring service some theologians have immediately seen substantial implications for the theology and practice of diaconate as these have developed over the last century and a half. Thus, in reviewing the book in *The Patristic and Byzantine Review* (1991), the well-known theologian, biblical scholar and ecumenist, John Reumann, who holds an interest in the Lutheran deaconess movement in the United States, used the word 'devastating' to describe the book's claim that the nineteenth-century renewal of the Lutheran diaconate in Germany was based on a false linguistic premise.

Similar reactions of concern were expressed within Anglican circles in the United States at a conference of the North American Association for the Diaconate in 1992. One can read these in the published conference papers edited by Peyton G. Craighill, *Diaconal Ministry, Past, Present and Future* (1994). Interestingly, a deacon of that church was about to publish a book on the diaconate when the publication of the linguistic study alerted him to the problems affecting the identity of the deacon as soon as one ceases to define the deacon in terms of loving and caring service. The author was Ormonde Plater, who then undertook the demanding task of revising his manuscript in the light of the proposed new linguistic insights into the meaning of the *diakon-* words. That this would have a profound effect on his understanding of the deacon in the church of today did not deter him. His book *Many Servants* was published nonetheless as early as 1991, and he has continued as an influential voice promoting this adjustment in the world of the Anglican diaconate.

The Hanover Report

Plater's book continues to be widely read, but Ormonde Plater has also contributed to ecumenical developments tied to the new linguistic information. In 1995 he was part of the Anglican representation working towards the new understandings of the diaconate that underlie the Hanover Report of the Anglican–Lutheran International Commission, *The Diaconate as Ecumenical Opportunity* (1996). Plater's reports on the progress of the consultation indicated that the consultation itself was taking stock of the relevance of the new linguistic information. When the Report duly appeared it did indeed acknowledge an indebtedness to 'the historical-philological corrective to earlier understandings of the *diakon-* words provided by Collins' *Diakonia*' (60). In fact, this book was the second of three sources listed as informing the reflections of the commission, the other two sources being the insights of the Faith and Order paper *Baptism, Eucharist, Ministry* (1982) and the church's tradition.

In the Church of England

Although the Hanover Report was not entirely consistent in drawing out implications of 'the historical–philological corrective', its acknowledgement of the new data and of the need for a rethinking of the diaconate has probably prompted other processes of revision. Within the Church of England itself stocktaking has been under way for some years. Sr Teresa Joan White has consistently drawn attention to the research in the newsletters she edits, *Distinctive Diaconate News* (for Anglican deacons) and *Diakonia News* (for the international organization of deacons and deaconesses, DIAKONIA). No. 86 of the latter (November 1999) reported on seminars and workshops on the material in which I was engaged in Uppsala, London and Bossey, Switzerland, during the summer of 1999. One of the workshops was under the auspices of the Diaconal Association of the Church of England, whose website (http://societies.anglican.org/dace/pub/index.html) has reported discussion and debate on issues emerging from the research. Here, in the association's newsletter of May 1997, Bishop Barry Rogerson of Bristol, a leading advocate of the research, issued a strong call for a renewal of language in relation to the identity and role of the distinctive or permanent deacon.

Subsequently, as the result of a motion to the General Synod of the Church of England in November 1998 from the Diocese of Ely, the synod established a Working Party of the House of Bishops to review the diaconate. The background paper of the previous October (General Synod Misc. 535) had endorsed the recommendation from the Ely Diocesan Synod of further study of my work as a process that 'may illuminate our Church's understanding of diaconal ministry'. Bishop Rogerson was to chair the working party whose report, *For such a time as this: A renewed diaconate in the Church of England*, appeared in October 2001 in preparation for debate in the General Synod of November 2001.

The report of some 70 pages was a succinct but wide-ranging appraisal of prior experience of the diaconate within the Church of England; of major factors contributing to an understanding of the identity and role of the ordained deacon; and of the pastoral potential of deacons within what it described as 'a largely post-Christian culture'. Factors contributing significantly to the review included the Church of England's understanding of church, ordination, liturgy, and mission; its ecumenical experience of diaconate, as in the Hanover Report; and its own distinctive but rich fabric of lay ministries. Nonetheless, the point of departure for a 'renewed diaconate' was what it called 'the recent rediscovery of the biblical idea of *diakonia*' (p. 9). Insights from this recent re-interpretation 'enable us to see the office of deacon in a new light' (p. 35). The resulting pastoral profile of the office of deacon, while challenging, is drawn against the background of realities of life in the Church of England, but consistently under the illumination of the 'new light'. Considerations in following sections of this book would support the strongly ecclesial connection which the report called for as well as much of the pastoral strategy it envisaged.

Nordic countries

Longstanding connections between the Church of England and the Church of Sweden have contributed to the development of their common interest in the research. Several publications in the United Kingdom as well as across Nordic countries provide clear evidence of these mutual interests. Since about 1995, in both countries, the theology of the diaconate has been subject to increasing scrutiny. One notices a shift of preoccupation between such earlier publications as the papers edited in England by Christine Hall in *The Deacon's Ministry* (1991) or those from Sweden in *Diakonetet i olika kyrkotraditioner* (The Diaconate in different church traditions 1995) and more recent publications from either country. Thus, in her contribution to a 1997 Swedish set of studies, *Diakonins teologi* (English version, *The Theology of Diaconia* 1999), Birgitta Laghé alerted readers to the existence of the linguistic research and to the scope of its relevance to the contemporary diaconate. In England, similarly, Robert Hannaford, a colleague of Christine Hall, with whom he edited *Order and Ministry* (1996), wrote of Collins' 'deconstruction of the ethical slant given to *diakonia* in the modern discussion of ministry' as 'a first step towards conceptual clarification'.

When these two churches undertook in 1997 to collaborate in a five-year Anglo-Nordic Diaconal Research Project (ANDREP), the focus on the re-interpretation of *diakonia* sharpened considerably. By the end of 1999 the group had already published a first collection of studies, *The Ministry of the Deacon: 1. Anglican–Lutheran Perspectives*, with a second appearing barely a year later, *The Ministry of the Deacon: 2. Ecclesiological Explorations*. Of interest here is how the first volume evidenced concern about 'the problem concerning the charitable character' of the diaconate which the new linguistic research exposed to view. Both Christine Hall in Britain and Sven-Erik Brodd in Sweden drew attention to the issue, the latter anticipating that 'this will be the focus of future debates'. Indeed, that same year Mats J. Hansson initiated such debate in a contribution to the Swedish journal *Tro & Tanke* (1999/2). Nonetheless, ANDREP's second volume significantly extended its reflections upon the relevance of the research. Brodd, on the one hand, insisted that *diakonia* could no longer be taken as mere charitable activity but was itself primarily an ecclesial responsibility arising from ordination. Hannaford, from the English side and a member of the Church of England Working Party whose report we have just considered, again explored 'the ecclesiological background to the concept of ministry' which the new research revealed. In addition, in a contribution to ANDREP2, 'The Diaconate: Ministry of Prophecy and Transformation', the Norwegian theologian Kjell Nordstokke constructed a dynamic vision of the diaconate as 'a power to invert values and relations'; informing this vision was an understanding of *diakonia* as 'conscious mission with divine authority and with the mandate to be a go-between in contexts of conflict and suffering'.

Ministry in general

As might be inferred from Robert Hannaford's interest in the ecclesiological dimensions of *diakonia*, theologians are insisting that the most fruitful way to advance consideration of the place of the diaconate in the church is to identify and describe its place within the ministry of the church. Inevitably any such considerations will have to be done within a yet broader view of *diakonia*, because that remains a leading theological indicator from our sources for ministry in the New Testament. Here too we have striking evidence of how some have perceived the relevance of the new research. In a definitive moment of his opening address to the 1990 Synod of Bishops in Rome on the Formation of Priests, Cardinal Ratzinger, Prefect of the Congregation for the Doctrine of the Faith, was expressing concern at what he interpreted as Protestant influences on the theology of priesthood. These influences would, in his view, diminish the traditional understanding of Catholic priesthood in so far as they worked towards presenting priesthood as a mere function within the community. The root cause of this development Ratzinger attributed to a mistaken understanding of the early Christian term for ministry, in particular, of the Greek word *diakonia*. At once he pointed out that the interpretation of this term which Protestant scholars had developed was erroneous, his grounds for this assessment being my doctoral thesis on which my linguistic study *Diakonia* published that year was based. (Ratzinger's address is published in English in a collection of his papers entitled *Called to Communion: Understanding the Church Today*, 1996).

Moving out

Such recourses to the new linguistic understanding of the *diakon-* words as we have been reviewing are acknowledgements on the part of a number of scholars and theological commissions that today's theology has not yet got the ancient *diakonia* right. Further, they would also be suggesting that theology needs to do just that if we are to be seen to be taking our biblical sources seriously. To date, newer reflections have indeed extended some theological horizons, but perhaps only the Anglo-Nordic Diaconal Research Project and the Working Party of the House of Bishops of the Church of England have moved towards resolving widely-acknowledged problems and ambiguities surrounding the theory and practice of diaconate. Elsewhere some groups and some individual theologians seem to be indicating that it would be unwise to commit the diaconate exclusively to a service of loving care when a body of research is indicating that the *diakon-* words themselves did not have that orientation in the early Christian era.

To flag a warning of such a situation is surely necessary. But equally important is to explore what the newly-revealed orientation of these words might be suggesting about the nature of the diaconate today. More than ten years ago, in the Afterword in my book *Diakonia*, I sketched some of this, but to my knowledge those ideas have not attracted particular comment. Nonetheless it would seem that if the new linguistic understanding of *diakonia* is enough to make students of the modern diaconate pause in the way they have been proceeding, it should also encourage some scouting and probing in other directions. At present the research marks a frontier. Frontiers, however, serve two purposes. These are, firstly, to be a safe barrier against unwelcome intrusions but then, secondly, to be a staging post for exploratory moves forward. Indications are that such moves are needed now.

Status quo

In contrast with those who seem ready to find ways forward are those who seem disinclined to disturb the present orientation of the diaconate. They might indeed acknowledge the new linguistic research. Thus the 1991 report to the Churchwide Assembly of the Evangelical Lutheran Church in America, *The Study of Ministry*, duly registered how the 'dominant understanding' had been 'challenged' by my 'thorough re-examination of the classical sources' (note 16; see also p. 40 with note 136); nonetheless, the Final Report of 1993 drew no implications at all for the diaconate when the report proceeded to formulate views at variance with the published research.

Again, the Louvain papers *Diaconat XX1ᵉ siècle* reveal little familiarity with the research. The historian of the early church, Alexandre Faivre, acknowledged the existence of 'an important body of biblical and non-biblical sources' relating to discussion about the diaconate, but proceeded to address problematical issues without reference to them. Hervé Legrand, on the other hand, did indeed briefly outline the nature of the published research and reported the challenge it presents to the idea of a diaconate of service, but in a stunningly brief rebuttal questioned the reliability of the linguistic enterprise without instancing a single philological item. Hardly more satisfactory is the brief handling of the new material in

Jeannine Olson's history of the diaconate, *One Ministry Many Roles* (1992), and in the revised edition of James Monroe Barnett's *The Diaconate: A Full and Equal Order* (1995). At least the latter occasioned debate between Barnett and myself in *Diakoneo* (1995/3 and 1996/2). Among Orthodox publications, *Women Deacons in the Orthodox Church* (1999) by Kyriaki Karidoyanes FitzGerald simply overrides the relevance of the research to the position of women within the diaconate (p. 108) but at the expense of misrepresenting it. One has difficulty seeing passing comment such as occurs in these publications as helpful ways to advance theological reflection on an issue which most confess is in need of further study.

On a different level is the problematic position which Andrew Clarke adopted in regard to the research in the concluding pages of *Serve the Community of the Church: Christians as Leaders and Ministers* (2000). The book provides an excellent resource in describing the rich and varied socio-religious background of leadership in the Graeco-Roman world of the first century CE and against this background seeks to describe the strongly contrasting style of early Christian leadership. In identifying the leading Christian characteristic as a profound sense of servanthood, Clarke has to declare a position in regard to my very different estimation of the place of the *diakon-* words in early Christian ministerial arrangements. In the light of the strong comparative linguistic base on which my semantic profile of the words is raised, I can only say here, much as I have said in regard to Legrand, that I find Clarke's contrary assertions defective, especially with respect to Paul's rhetoric in 1 and 2 Corinthians, where scholarly exegesis has welcomed my contribution. With respect to Clarke's reservations about my treatment of the *diakon-* words in the synoptic tradition, I see no reason to revise my judgement, as, indeed, my exposition in the following chapter 2 will illustrate.

More common than such inconsequential references to the new research, however, are presentations which proceed without reference to it at all. A striking instance would be the large collection of papers, edited by Peter Hünermann and colleagues, from the congress on women deacons held in Stuttgart in April 1997, *Diakonat: Ein Amt für Frauen* ... (Diaconate: An office for women ...) Equally significant, both by reason of its author, Gerhard Müller, a member of the Roman Catholic International Theological Commission which engaged in a review of the diaconate in 2001, and because it argues in a contrary direction, is *Priestertum und Diakonat* (Priesthood and Diaconate, 2000). Müller seeks to deepen the theological grounds for a male only priesthood and proceeds to press similar arguments for the exclusion of women from diaconate. Once his theological abstractions concerning exclusive gender roles and an inbuilt orientation of diaconate to priesthood are exposed to the implications of the ancient *diakonia*, however, his arguments would be difficult to sustain. In spite of the close critique Müller engages in regard to Dorothea Reininger's work of 1999 (soon to be noted), he himself, unlike her, appears to be unaware of the existence of the new research.

Both the Hünermann and Müller volumes have been German exercises and, with the interesting exception of Dorothea Reininger's study, and of Ute Eisen's passing acknowledgement in her historical investigation of women office-bearers, their silence in regard to the new research characterizes virtually all writing on the diaconate in German, whether Roman Catholic, Lutheran or Reformed. To my knowledge there was no scholarly German review of the book *Diakonia: Re-interpreting the Ancient Sources*. This contrasts with widely-spread reviews in Britain and the United States, and with a review in the leading biblical journal in France, *Revue biblique*. Numbers of these reviews speak of the research to the effect that it is 'indispensable' for addressing questions of ministry.

Given the existence in Germany, on the Roman Catholic side, of an International Centre for the Diaconate, and on the Lutheran side of a Scientific Diakonia Institute at the

University of Heidelberg, their silence in regard to the new research is mystifying. In the decade since the publication of my book, the journal *Theologische Rundschau*, which publishes surveys of significant developments across theological fields, has published two surveys of research into *Diakonie* (to use the German word) with neither of these having noted the existence of the new lexical description of *diakonia*. In fact, the more recent of the two surveys by Peter Bloth (2001) actually drew attention to the need for a work which might present a study of *diakonia* in the light both of modern biblical scholarship and of the word's broader cultural background. Ironically, the reviewer claimed to find this need met by numerous studies in the volume by Schäfer and Strohm referred to earlier, whereas these studies merely repeated the traditional German Lutheran understanding of *diakonia* as a lowly loving service.

Similar neglect of the new lexical description has also characterized the reflections by Margaret Crain and Jack Seymour on the new United Methodist diaconate of the United States contained in *A Deacon's Heart* (2001), as well as Roman Catholic attitudes in the broad diaconal circles of the United States, which is the more surprising in that this country witnessed considerable scholarly interest in the book and continues to provide evidence of scholarly approval of the book in biblical circles. Thus, a chapter directed at current questions about the diaconate in Susan K. Wood's *Sacramental Orders* (2000) was completely silent in regard to the research. Instead of addressing issues relevant to the diaconate that have arisen from the research, the chapter addresses issues that have become problematical because the research has been neglected. The series of arguments for a female diaconate which Phyllis Zagano developed in *Holy Saturday* (2001) labours under a similar disadvantage. In arguing for 'diaconal ministry' without clarifying what its 'diaconal' character might be, Zagano works from loosely framed linguistic premises in regard to statements in the New Testament and without reference to the recent linguistic research on these matters.

Dorothea Reininger

Dorothea Reininger's scholarly study is singular among German writings on the diaconate in paying some attention to the new research. An extensive study (736 pages) published in 1999, *Diakonat der Frau in der Einen Kirche* (Women deacons in the one church) has as its object to put a strong case for the ordination of Roman Catholic women deacons. The study provides extensive surveys of historical developments, theologies, and pastoral practice in regard to female deacons across history and the ecumenical field before turning to the case for ordaining Roman Catholic women. At this well-developed stage of her work (p. 604), Reininger reflects on the diaconate as integral to the single sacrament of order before presenting 'the identity of the diaconate' in preparation for mounting her conclusions in regard to women's rightful place within the ordained diaconate.

The section on identity is thus important to her case, but develops to a predictable pattern as it revisits the sources of German understandings of the Greek *diakon-* words in Kittel's *Theological Dictionary of the New Testament*. The diaconate emerges as especially responsible for 'caritative care' in the church and has the capacity of 'diakonizing' the whole of the church's ministry. In such a process the role of women could well be determinative.

This is the strongly diakonic context within which Reininger introduces the new lexical understanding of *diakonia* presented in my book of 1990. In taking account of the new research, however, Reininger presents only one aspect of the semantic profile of *diakonia* as I described it. This is the aspect represented in the idea of the deacon as 'go-between or bridge'. She ventures to show that historically some element of the go-between has always been observable in practice, as when deacons acted as intermediaries between bishops and their communities, or when modern deacons have sought to establish connections between the local church and the social margins where they work.

From the standpoint of my research, however,

Reininger's attempt to accommodate the new linguistic data is misconceived. The idea of the go-between which she seeks to draw upon is only one part of the semantic compound making up the ancient *diakonia*; even so, this singular aspect of go-between formed no part of any notion of loving service such as Reininger still wants *diakonia* to represent. In addition, her study neglects to take into account those other aspects of the ancient *diakonia* which the research claims to be the real indicators of the identity of the deacon and which will be the object of review in the pages to follow.

Purpose

The present book aims principally to provide deacons with a reflective tour of writings from the New Testament and other early Christian literature which are commonly associated in deacons' minds with the diaconate. The line taken in some of the reflections will be different from what most of today's deacons are accustomed to. In such cases I will not necessarily alert the reader to the change, nor will I be entering into debate with other scholars. I propose simply to reflect on the meaning of passages that have had a direct appeal to deacons during the period of the renewal of the diaconate. Deacons – and their teachers – will thus have at their disposal a resource of early documentation that is presented in the light of the most recent linguistic research. The presentation aims to serve both an exegetical and a pastoral purpose. Readers will be spared the labour of working through the kind of argumentations which were required in establishing the meaning of some passages in *Diakonia: Re-interpreting the Ancient Sources* and in a number of other publications listed in the appendix. The concluding reflections will be a contribution to the continuing exploration of a theology of the diaconate.

2

The Diakonia of Jesus and the Early Church

The gospels appeal strongly to deacons because they abound with stories of Jesus freeing those who are victims of powerful forces. Jesus restores sight to those who cannot see, Jesus accepts the rejected, and Jesus displays in his deeds God's goodwill at work in the world. According to the scene Luke presents at the prophetic beginning of Jesus' ministry in Galilee (Luke 4:18–19), this is also what that community of Christians was taught about Jesus. And this is the programme which deacons set themselves today. The programme pulses with the Spirit which Jesus claimed for himself on that same occasion in Luke's narrative – 'The Spirit of the Lord is upon me' – and it requires of deacons the kind of service which their training instilled and which all the literature about deacons describes.

In the books and articles which deacons read, such activity is often presented as *diakonia*, and for deacons to participate in it is presented as sharing in the *diakonia* of Jesus. They do this by acting as a *diakonos* or servant of those in need. Occasionally in stories about Jesus at his work – but only occasionally – we actually encounter in the Greek gospels these deacon words. Naturally, given the central place which the prevailing understanding of these words has contributed to what we think a deacon is, stories and sayings of Jesus which use words like *diakonia* have provided deacons with much scope for reflection.

In the following selection of passages from the gospels and from other writings in the New Testament we will revisit such passages to read them in the light of perceptions of *diakonia* which are possible now that we have more detailed information about what *diakonia* meant in the ancient world. We will be looking for values which deacons in particular but others also may wish to take from each passage for their reflection and their own living.

The diakonia of the Son of Man

Mark 10:45 *'The Son of Man came to carry out his mission and give his life as a ransom for many.'*
One of the most powerful influences in establishing the servant model of deacon is a group of teachings in the gospels which make connections between disciples and servants. The most striking piece of teaching in this group occurs in Mark's gospel and is actually about Jesus himself, but at this point of the narrative the teaching about Jesus is prompted by what Jesus has just been teaching the disciples. Deacons have probably reflected on this passage of the scriptures more than on any other, just as they have heard bishops, theologians and fellow deacons deliver homilies, lectures and exhortations more on this passage than on any other. The passage is of course the one presenting Jesus as the Son of Man who has come not to be served but to serve and give his life as a ransom (Mark 10:45).

Breaking the sentence in two
Deacons will recall that when speakers use this verse from Mark's gospel to form the basis of what they want to say about the identity and role of the deacon more often than not they use the first part only. They will say, 'The Son of Man came not to be served but to serve', and they will make it sound as if it is a statement that stands on its own.

They are, however, leaving off the rest of Mark's statement, '... and to give his life as a ransom for many'. Dividing the statement into two parts in this way certainly makes the first part a very convenient tool with which to shape a model of a servant deacon. It is Jesus himself who speaks, he appears to be casting himself in a servant role, and the statement is ultimately directed at disciples because it forms the climax of teaching to disciples. In particular Jesus is linking the standard by which he has lived with the standard required of disciples by means of words about service which Mark expressed in Greek by *diakon-*. As all deacons know, their very title in the church is *diakonos*, which is the Greek noun. In the statement about Jesus serving, Mark used active and passive forms of the related verb *diakonein*.

Many writers on the diaconate and many official church statements present this part of the saying of Jesus as an open-and-shut case for the servant model which has determined the course of the development of the various diaconates in today's churches. By contrast, the first thing which a close examination of Mark 10:45 makes us realize is that the saying must be treated as a whole. There is no independent part (a), 'The Son of Man came not to be served but to serve.' There are two reasons for saying this. One arises from what we have come to understand about the way this particular Greek word for serving works in sentences, and the other relates to the structure of this particular sentence.

Keeping the sentence whole

We will consider the structure of the sentence first. Even before interpreters had become fully aware of the meanings which this serving word can carry, they realized that the so-called part (a) was to be understood only in relation to the second half or part (b) of the statement. That is, we are not in a position to understand what kind of service Jesus is referring to until we read part (b), 'and give his life as a ransom for many'. Thus we are to understand that the service of Jesus consists in giving his life as a ransom. It is not service of any other kind.

Commonly preachers – at times even translators and commentators – tell us that in this statement Jesus is saying that he came to serve people. One English Bible actually reads: 'to help people'. As a result we are invited to envisage those nameless suffering and distressed people who crowd around Jesus in so many gospel stories and receive health and solace. And on the basis of this kind of service, deacons are urged to commit themselves to a similar involvement with the suffering and distressed people of their societies. They are assured that this would give their diaconate the authentic character of the service or *diakonia* of Jesus.

We are not permitted, however, to read the statement in this way at all. An understanding of standard patterns of language explains why. It will also show us that, at the end of what we are calling part (a), people are not the recipients of the service. In fact there are no people in sight, and whatever kind of service this statement is attributing to Jesus it is not a service to people. The two phrases of part (a) and part (b) are linked by 'and' in a way that enables the second part to clarify what kind of service the speaker had in mind in the first part. This is a common pattern of speech in situations where the first part of a statement expresses itself through a word without a referent or which is indeterminate in meaning. We all make such statements frequently.

An illustration of the pattern in English would be the following: 'she was determined to serve again and make the company profitable'. On reading that sentence, it is not until we pick up clues from the words 'company' and 'profitable' that we are in a position to know the type of service which the individual is determined to undertake. From those clues we come to perceive that she was a strong-minded businesswoman, and that the type of service she intended to provide would consist in business management. Change a word or two and we arrive at another kind of service. Reading 'comfortable' instead of 'profitable', for instance, we enter a different situation: 'She was determined to serve and make the company comfortable'. We are now in a reception room or a restaurant, and we are encountering an embarrassed host or waitress who is determined to repair the damage done by someone's *faux pas* or by an accident with the soup.

Manufacturing a theology of service

We can learn a little more about this common pattern of language by contrasting it with another pattern formed around 'and'. In this second pattern the significant word in the first part of a statement does have a referent, that is, does identify a specific situation. Thus, 'she was determined to serve out her term and begin a new venture.' Here 'and' is simply coupling two discrete actions whose only relationship to one another is that they are to be performed in sequence. We clearly perceive each action for what it is.

This is the way many people are reading Jesus' saying at Mark 10:45. Consequently they think Mark was writing of two separate activities of Jesus, one referring to his work of service among people and the other referring to the offering of his life. The two parts would refer to discrete activities performed in sequence, one in the course of his public ministry and the other on the cross.

Given the broad acceptance of such an understanding of Mark 10:45, some are drawn to speculate theologically on the connection between two such aspects of Jesus' ministry. In fact, some of this speculation colours reflections on the theological character of the ministry of deacons. It does so in the following way: in extending selfless and loving service to those in need, deacons would be extending across time the *diakonia* of Jesus by which he brought redemption to the world.

Getting back to the meaning of a word

Deacons may be interested to know that some such theological connection between these so-called parts of Mark
10:45 was what attracted me to the study of *diakonia* in the
first place. Mark's verse appeared to me at the time to offer
rich possibilities for deepening an appreciation of the
nature of ordained ministry, opening up its *Jesus-power*.

Attractive as such a hypothesis may have been,
however, its windows of opportunity closed once a study
of how ancient Greeks used the *diakon-* words revealed
that the service Jesus was speaking of was indeterminate.
In other words, Jesus' statement in the so-called part (a)
about coming to serve cannot be understood until we read
part (b), where we discover that his service is to give his
life as a ransom for many. The pattern of this statement is,
then, the same as the pattern we considered above about
the business woman 'determined to serve *and* make the
company profitable', where *and* introduces the few words
explaining the kind of service she is offering. In such cases,
we need clues from the rest of the sentence before we
know of what the service consists.

Identifying the diakonia of Jesus

This leads to another observation about the structure of this
saying attributed to Jesus in Mark. We have been referring
to part (a) and understanding it to contain the words 'The
Son of Man came not to be served but to serve'. Since the
meaning of such a statement is incomplete or at least
obscure, we would be much better advised to restructure
the sentence in a different way. This restructuring makes
the following words part (1): 'The Son of Man came not to be
served'. We will look at this new part (1) in the following
section. For now, part (2) of the sentence would become:
'but to serve and give his life as a ransom for many'. With
the sentence restructured in this way, part (2) is self-
contained and conveys a full and free-standing idea: 'the
Son of man came to serve by giving his life as a ransom for
many'. (Grammarians have a word for this kind of 'and' in

a sentence; they call it *epexegetical,* and by that they mean that 'and' introduces the part of the sentence which explains or clarifies the part preceding 'and'.)

The only other thing in Mark's famous sentence requiring further clarification is the question about who it is that the Son of Man is serving. The answer is not far away. The whole of Mark's narrative is about the answer to that question. At his death the centurion said, 'Truly, this man was God's son'. That is, the same Son as the voice from heaven proclaimed at his baptism at the beginning of the narrative, 'You are my son, my loved son: I take my delight in you'. The gospel Mark writes follows the Son's path from one proclamation of his identity to another because that was the path of the Son's calling. It was also the path which the disciples and the Markan community were called to follow. The *diakonia* of Jesus, as dramatically contextualized by Mark in chapter 10, at the end of the Galilean mission and on the road to Jerusalem, was to serve the One whose voice called to him at his baptism, and the Son of Man would perform this service by carrying out the mission to which that voice had consecrated him.

This picture of the *diakonia* of Jesus is what Mark thought we would make of his carefully constructed scene. That is how he understood the service of Jesus in this statement. No ancient Greek would have had a problem arriving at this understanding. Certainly Mark had no worries about the statement not being clear enough. In fact he would be very surprised to find us getting confused about it.

Mark 10:45 *'The Son of Man did not come to have attendants waiting on him.'*
If we accept this as the gist of what Mark meant to say in part (2) of this pivotal statement about the mission of the Son of Man, what are we to make of part (1) of the statement, 'The Son of Man came not to be served'? What kind of service is this? Here again, for the ancient Greek there would have been no problem, and indeed the context

eases even the reader of a modern translation into its meaning. The writing is in fact very effective.

Realities of life

The immediate context has been an argument among disciples as they followed Jesus along the road from Galilee to Jerusalem. After James and John have sought high places beside Jesus in his glory, the other ten complain of the arrogance and self-seeking of these two. Jesus' response is forceful, and sets the tone and imagery for what issues at verse 45 in his statement about service. Let us look into the first part of his response.

To disciples under an illusion of impending grandeur, as the story presents James and John as having been – 'one at your right and one at your left' (Mark 10:37) – the teacher gives a sharp reminder of the realities of life.

In the mention by Jesus of the government (verse 42: let us think of grasping Roman representatives of an absolute despot in the Emperor Tiberius and most of his successors in the first century), of 'great men' (let us envisage grossly conspicuous consumers and rapacious exploiters), of how they 'lord it over people' (disdaining what we call individual rights), and lastly – the most terrible of all – of 'authority' (read an easy disregard for life and property when it comes to an issue of who rules the day), we glimpse a Mediterranean world where wealth of an enormous scale resided in an élite comprising little more than 1 per cent of the population. Among the masses, 30 per cent were slaves, while the rest were either unemployed in metropolitan centres like Alexandria and Antioch or were being ground down under imperial imposts and by labour in the fields from dawn to dusk to try and keep ahead of debt to landlords and religious authorities.

A small middle class of civil servants and merchants experienced some sense of security, but their interest and indeed their social obligation lay in aping the style of the impossibly rich in the pursuit, at any cost, of the most precious possession the ancient Mediterranean world had

to offer. This was honour. Honour was the public perception that one owned cash, property and slaves, and could
entertain expectations of recognition within the great
Empire of the divine Caesar of the hour. With honour came
the correlating obligation to despise the general populace.

A different kind of honour

Jesus said:

> You know how those supposed to govern the Gentiles
> lord it over them,
> and their great men exert authority over them;
> but this is not your way.
> Instead, whoever wants to be great among you will be
> your servant,
> and whoever wants to be first among you will be every
> one's slave.

Let us recall that Jesus is speaking to two men who think
Jesus is taking them on the road to what they call his
'glory'. By 'glory' we are to understand 'honour' here, a
level of honour unparalleled even by the legendary
honour of emperors.

Jesus' opening comment – 'this is not your way' –
brusquely disillusions anyone living in hope of honour. A
new kind of society opens before those who have been
harbouring visions of a share in imperial greatness. In
terms of social reward and personal satisfaction the
panorama is bleak. It is empty of the timeless symbols of
upward mobility, dignity and success. The contrast
between the political and social realities of the first
century and the conditions of being within a discipleship
of the Son of Man is absolute. So absolute in fact that there
is no point of contact between them.

In contrasting the lordship of the great men with conditions within the discipleship the sayings are not presenting a sociological spectrum, with the emperor at one end
of a continuum and slaves at the other. Rather, the sayings

present an alternative way of looking at life. Instead of passing from one glorious end of the social spectrum to another which is extremely less comfortable and privileged, the sayings make a switch from the Roman empire to a totally different realm, to a kingdom not of this world, where awful power and glowing honour are not factors at work. Over against the war, taxes, trade and wealth of Rome stands a realm of discipleship. Within the realm of discipleship operate forces unknown to emperors and military champions. These are the life-forces within parables which tell of a young man reaching a solitary decision to leave a messy life behind (Luke 15:17–18); the tumultuous inner revolutions within the woman embracing Jesus (Luke 7:38); the courage to drink the cup which he will drink (Mark 10:38).

Empire and discipleship

The clue to the meaning of these sayings about the nature of discipleship is in such sets of contrasts. The sayings of course put the contrasts in a condensed form, and are the more effective for that. And it would be a mistake on our part to take just one word out of this context, which is both complex and dense, and allow its supposed values to dictate the message of the teacher here. Rather, the teaching is to emerge from the context of the passage and from the alternative values which the teacher dangles before obtuse followers.

After the descriptive allusions to the ways of this world, the teacher deftly contrasts the dominant values of the two realms of empire and of discipleship within the Kingdom of God:

EMPIRE	DISCIPLESHIP
great	*servant*
first	*slave*

The simple diagram, read with the text of Mark 10:43–44 and within the context we have just set, shows that the words 'servant' and 'slave' are introduced into the sayings for the purpose of identifying the extreme contrast between two social groups. The two words stand opposed to 'great' and 'first'. The imperial group pursues values which are immediately recognizable and which have been part of our historical understanding and of folklore from time immemorial. But the sayings of Jesus are insisting that discipleship does not operate by the principles which make one 'great' or 'first'. Instead discipleship operates by principles which no social organization has ever known; or rather, the sayings are proposing that discipleship is not a sociological function at all. The contrast with empire is indicating that discipleship functions at a level where power does not exist. The situation is not only that power is inappropriate within discipleship, but that discipleship is an environment which is not receptive of power.

The two words 'servant' and 'slave' are indicating that discipleship – the preferred term in the gospel tradition is Kingdom of God – opens up a different plane of existence where the style and interplay of social forces have no relevance. One term is of no more significance than the other. The fact that one of them is the Greek word *diakonos* ('servant') does not give it greater significance than the other (*doulos*: 'slave') because *diakonos* has no reference to later functions within a settled ecclesiastical establishment. It is wholly unlikely that anyone in the audience for whom Mark was writing knew what a deacon/*diakonos* was; what is more, the sayings were circulating in Christian circles well before Mark composed his gospel, in a period certainly predating the existence of people we call deacons. The term servant/*diakonos* in this saying is just a complementary expression to the term slave/*doulos*, just one word beside another to illustrate that the Kingdom of God is not a political playground and is not to be defiled by ambition, greed, and oppressive surges of power.

A string of sayings

This understanding of the sayings in one of Mark's most significant passages is confirmed by a consideration of sayings of a similar character which occur elsewhere in the gospel tradition. One of these occurs in a situation not unlike that of the ambitions of James and John. The disciples 'had argued with one another who was the greatest' (Mark 9:34), and Jesus 'summoned the Twelve' – a sign that Mark is considering issues of discipleship as they affect leaders in the community – and told them (9:35):

'If anyone wants to be *first*, let him be *last* of all and *servant/diakonos* of all.'

At Matthew 23:11 we read:

'he who is *greatest* among you will be your *servant/diakonos*.'

At Luke 9:48:

'the *lowliest* among you all, he is truly *great*.'

This string of similar sayings reveals how deeply the teaching they contained permeated the tradition. These sayings are linked not only with one another but also with teaching which uses children as points of reference to the nature of the Kingdom of God. At Mark 9:36 (similarly at Luke 9:47) Jesus moves on from rebuking the Twelve to 'set a little child in the centre of their circle', and 'taking him in his arms', said to the Twelve:

'Whoever receives one of such children in my name receives me.'

The introduction of the little child into the equation tells us much about the teaching expressed in the sayings about the lowliest, the last, the slave and the servant. The little child does not participate in decisions which affect the shape of the adult world and yet, powerless, flourishes in the relationship of love and dependence with its parents. Incapable of deploying power, the child enjoys the fullness of life, and becomes another illustration of the paradox of the Kingdom.

The richest experience

All the sayings are teaching disciples that in accepting a place in the Kingdom, members of the community are to abandon processes by which societies operate. Instead they are to stand in relationships with God and with one another in a community of discipleship. The sayings are not a call to abstain from the management of affairs or to eschew the responsibility of authority. They are a call, however, to recognize that the management of affairs and the deployment of authority are activities of this world whereas the Kingdom of God establishes itself in a community of relationships. The community will no longer provide communion when power distorts the dynamism of relationships.

In giving expression to this teaching the sayings have occasion to draw on the word *diakonos*. There is nothing special in this choice. The term does not contribute anything more specific to the discussion than what is already conveyed about qualities required in disciples by the other terms *last, lowliest,* and *slave.* The expression *servant/diakonos* is just another in the series of analogies which the sayings build. As the child is the most immature of the human community, so within the great house the servant is the most powerless. And as the child has the richest experience of love and security, so the Kingdom reveals its wealth and power where there is the recognition of the least claim to it. We will see further reaches of this teaching in Luke's presentation of the Lord as the community's enduring friend.

The community's enduring friend

Luke 22:27 *'I am in your midst as one who waits on you.'*

Deacons reflecting on the mission of the Son of Man as expressed at Mark 10:45 will eventually be led to reflect on the scene of the Last Supper in which Luke also presents Jesus speaking of himself as a servant by using a *diakon-*

word. Although fifty years ago there was much scholarly discussion of the relationship between these two passages from the gospels of Mark and Luke, in my view there can be no doubt at all that the character of Luke's passage is a result of Luke's decision to recontextualize Mark's passage about the Son of Man which we have just been considering. Luke was thoroughly familiar with this passage in Mark and recognized its importance.

Reworking Mark

Of course in speaking like this I am taking for granted that Luke used Mark as a source. In doing so I am aware that in recent years some scholars have been arguing against the standard working hypothesis of relationships between the synoptic gospels of Matthew, Mark and Luke. The instance of literary relationships between Luke and Mark which we are about to touch on in what follows has long led me to feel at ease working with the hypothesis.

As I hope readers will discover, ancient texts like these speak more authentically and reveal surprising layers of meaning the closer we are able to analyse them. After all, their authors were not just writing stories or memoirs. The short works we call gospels – Mark is only about 11,000 words – were closely considered in their composition, and the compositions are best read as narrative theology. The expression is not to be misunderstood. Theology is the key word.

As noted above, the passage about the Son of Man occurs in Mark as Jesus moves along the road to Jerusalem with his followers. In Luke, by contrast, the passage occurs when Jesus and the disciples have been in Jerusalem for about a week and are reclining at the Passover meal on the night Jesus is to be betrayed. Luke has set this scene with care. After precise instructions for the preparation for the Passover, Jesus declares the value to him of having them all gathered at the Passover table: 'I have longingly desired to eat this Passover with you before I suffer'. The sharing of the bread and wine follows. Then, differing from Mark and Matthew, the narrative does not move directly to the events leading to the arrest of Jesus but pauses while Jesus delivers a discourse to the disciples.

The discourse consists of pieces of teaching which have each had a place somewhere else in other gospel narratives. The dispute about greatness at the Passover table in Luke 22:24–27 clearly must stand in some kind of relationship to the dispute recorded by Mark prior to Jesus' arrival in Jerusalem (Mark 10:35–45). We will consider that. Following the dispute we have Jesus endorsing the status of the apostles within the Kingdom – a title carefully nurtured by Luke (6:13; 22:14) to ensure that his own community strove to remain faithful to what he later calls 'the apostles' teaching and fellowship' (Acts 2:42). In this part of the short discourse, however, Luke has constructed this teaching on the basis of some teachings which he held in common with Matthew (Q) and which Matthew used prior to Jesus' arrival in Jerusalem (Matthew 19:28). Next, in Luke, still at the table, Jesus addresses both a warning and a reassurance to Simon Peter; by contrast, in Mark this prediction of Peter's denial occurs on the walk from the Passover room to the Mount of Olives. After addressing Simon Peter, Jesus delivers instructions to the apostles about preparedness for flight. These echo earlier instructions about the urgency of the mission, as at Luke 9:3. In other words, throughout Jesus's discourse after the Passover we encounter little original material, and I believe Luke has put the discourse together from a variety of sources for the reason that he wanted to present a discourse from the master at a meal with his disciples before the master was snatched from his intimate circle.

A Hellenistic artist
Luke was a thoroughly Hellenized literary artist, although the material he was dealing with in the gospel tradition did not provide him with many opportunities to display the skills and tastes which he had developed within his Greek culture. Nonetheless, in several ways Luke indi-

cates that he was aware he was addressing people of his own kind. In the eyes of this Hellenistic audience Luke's scene of the final – if temporary! – separation of master and disciples at the end of a special meal would not be complete without a farewell address from the master teacher. In addition, in the interests of this Hellenistic audience the scene had to suggest the convention of the Greek dinner followed by its symposion.

Technically the symposion was a function distinct from the dinner, although it was only a prolongation of the dinner gathering and was conducted in the same room. Interestingly, an additional guest list might operate at this point, with people invited to share in the wine while the more stimulating and perhaps learned participants displayed their skills and wisdom for the admiration and betterment of all. On particular occasions a significant individual would be expected to hold the attention of the rest of the gathering. And this, of course, is the effect Luke creates here.

So it is that Jesus discourses on the nature of the Kingdom, of which Luke has made a feature in his whole presentation of Jesus. Luke has presented Jesus as born to sit on the throne of his ancestor David (1:32) and, on his entry to the city where David had reigned, has the crowd shouting, 'Blessed is the king who comes in the name of the Lord' (19:38). Each of the other gospels also includes an acclamation of Jesus as he enters Jerusalem, but they do not insert the word 'king' into this line from one of the pilgrim songs in the Book of Psalms (Psalm 118:26). The theme of Jesus' kingly status Luke builds into the discourse after he has presented his version of the dispute about greatness. Jesus acknowledges the fidelity of the disciples and assures them of their place in the Kingdom which his Father has assigned to him (22:28–30). Even in the report of the dispute, the emphasis is less on the nature of the conflict between the disciples than on the lordly manner in which Jesus resolves it. This is the true mark of the wise leader.

With other touches of detail Luke Hellenizes Mark's address. Mark's phrase about those who were 'supposed to govern the Gentiles' becomes 'the kings of the Gentiles', to suit his readers' familiarity with a Hellenistic flowering of kingdoms, while the executors of royal decrees become 'benefactors'. These men were wealthy governors and other senior appointees of whom their Hellenistic clientele expected grandiose public works and civic amenities. Such a Lukan world generated honour for the benefactors, an honour of which Luke's readers were vividly aware and of which they stood in awe.

Next, moving to the resolution of the dispute, and closely following at this stage the lines of teaching in Mark's roadside scene, Luke changes Mark's images to suit the setting of his Hellenistic dinner and symposion. Instead of having Jesus overturn the value system of royal honours and public esteem through the use of Mark's contrasts between rulers and slaves, Luke shifts to contrasts between the esteemed host of a Hellenistic dinner and those attending on him and his guests.

> The most senior among you must become like the junior,
> and the presider must become like the one attending at the table.
>
> Who is greater, the one reclining in the main place
> or the one attending on him?
>
> Nonetheless, I am here in your midst like one who is attending at the tables.

Appropriate words for a symposion

Here 'the one attending at the tables' is expressed in the Greek not by the noun *diakonos* in the sense of 'the waiter' but by the present participle *diakonōn* (hence the English participle 'attending' in the translation). The use of the participle is another detail of Hellenistic literary style. In reporting waiters at work, Greek writers preferred the participle to the noun as giving a more immediate sense of the waiter in action. That stylistic detail is another small reminder that Luke's priority in this scene, for the purposes of developing its teaching, is to thoroughly Hellenize it. Hence also his use of the *diakon-* words. We need to take note of the significance of their presence in this scene. Their presence is to be explained on the basis of Greek literary convention.

Throughout the twentieth century commentators regularly claimed that the *diakon-* words were, to use the often repeated phrase, ordinary everyday words. Then, given their prominent place in the language which early Christians chose for the purpose of designating activities and roles in the early church – the title 'deacon' is itself one illustration – commentators have gone on to propose that the very ordinariness of the words underlay the choice. In this, early Christians would have been flagging a rejection of the high language of temples and public office, pompous and even intimidating as these could be in the flamboyant world of Hellenistic religions. In fact commentators have traced the early Christian preference for *diakon-* words to the ordinariness of Jesus' own everyday contact with people of very ordinary stations in life – and of no station at all. At such a level, we are told, the language of the streets was more appropriate. Accordingly, if later Christian leaders were to be servants of their congregations in the way that Jesus said he was a servant among his own, then what better title for leaders and for roles within the community than terms taken from slavish language like the *diakon-* words.

Luke knew better than this, however. He knew what has only become apparent through a few linguistic studies over recent decades. Luke knew that Greek writers used *diakon-* words for waiters at table almost exclusively in formal language and in composing accounts of formal meals. To this we need to add the fact that for the Greek any meal, but inevitably the formal meal, was a religious act, as it so often is in other cultures. The style of the formal Greek meal and the expectations attending it are not to be confused with the laxities and extravagances of Roman feasts. Among the Greeks the first action of a gathering was to invoke the presence of the gods and then honour their presence with a ritual libation of wine. The occasion was ideally of such dignity and religious significance that Athenaeus, an apologist of conventions applying to these occasions, observed that the table attendants could not be slaves. The presence of such unworthy functionaries would be abhorrent to the gods and would drive away the divine presences. Thus, in Luke's simple narrative of the Lord's Supper, values abound in the code words he introduces and in the sensitivities to the occasion that he betrays.

On another level

Luke is advising his audience that this meal, with which they were thoroughly familiar from their own community practice of remembering the Lord in the breaking of bread, is a moment of sacred encounter. And in constructing the scene, and in reporting the discourse relating to the dispute among the disciples, Luke has carefully modified the account he has inherited from Mark in order to help his Hellenistic audience recognize something more than a loving meal and a sad farewell. In the account of this last meeting between disciples and the Lord before he suffers, Luke has elevated to another level the simple, if challenging, ethic inculcated by Mark's story about the dispute among the disciples along the road.

In Luke's treatment, similarly to Mark's, the Kingdom – even the King – does not function according to the protocols and pretences of the self-promoting seekers of power in public life. But Luke goes beyond Mark in having his Hellenistic audience read the signs that the Kingdom functions only by reason of the constant presence of the community before the Lord. Luke's intention is to cultivate the community's awareness of the Lord's presence in it. 'I am in your midst like one who is attending at the tables.' This is the point of the resolution of the dispute in Jesus' discourse. Disputes must end because the Lord is 'in the midst'.

With the resolution of the dispute, the discourse immediately opens upon the promise of Kingdom. As beneficiaries of that promise, they shall eat and drink 'at my table in my kingdom' (22:30). Until then, however, the community table is the place of encounter. To create the conviction of that possibility among his readers Luke has shaped his narrative, even to the point of the *diakon-* word. Luke's choice of this word is not the result of casual usage. Nor is its presence in the narrative for the purpose of inculcating lessons about lowly service by one member of a community to another. The only reason Luke uses the word is so that it will contribute to the dignity of the occasion. As a minor stylistic feature *diakon-* is recognizable to Luke's readers as marking the formal and religious nature of the occasion.

All days

Something else would also have been recognizable to Luke's readers about a master and lord who waits on his dependants at table. In the slave-based economy of the Roman empire – and indeed of the earlier Greek economy – annual festivals were known to all in which wealthy heads of households organized peers to assist them in providing a feast for the slave-born members of their often vast establishments. A major instance was the Roman Saturnalia, but smaller regional versions are also known. Such is the tone of Luke's presentation of the Lord's Supper, however, that one is justified in suspecting that Luke is playing off one institution against another: the public festivals against the intimacy of the Lord's table – to the advantage of the latter, of course.

We have emphasized how a close consideration of the discourse of Jesus after the meal leads to a realization that Luke is speaking of the presence of the Lord at all Christian ritual. But this kind of teaching is not confined to the account of the Lord's Supper. Throughout his gospel Luke has immersed readers in persistent teaching about the ongoing presence of the Lord in gatherings around the table as well as about dangers attendant upon neglecting the opportunities which such gatherings provide (4:39; 5:30; 5:34; 7:36–48; 9:12–17; 10:38–42; 12:35–40; 14:7–14; 14:15–24; 15:20–32; 15:19–23; 19:1–10). In addition there is a dynamism in the presence, which Luke evokes. When it is the Lord who gathers a people in a household, one could indeed say, 'salvation has come to this household today' (19:9).

In the gatherings of Luke's community its members were to understand that the saving and healing activity of Jesus was extending to their day – and then beyond into the future of the church. Luke signals this conviction in the way he brings a definitive close to the gospel as a whole on the basis of the meal between two doubting disciples and the risen Lord at Emmaus. He next proceeds to project the theme into the story of the church (Acts 2:42; 3:43–47). His aim is to remind the church that thus it will always be. The superiority over the Saturnalia of such persistent teaching about a confirming and ongoing presence of the Lord is clear. The Saturnalia was a day off for slaves. Luke's Christian community has the Lord in its midst all days.

The role of the Seven

Acts 6:3 *'Select seven men full of Spirit and wisdom'*
Deacons have constantly been inspired by the story of the seven Greek men who were presented to the apostles who, in turn, 'prayed and laid their hands on them' (Acts 6:6). Tradition has seen in these men, and in particular in the most famous of them, Stephen, the forerunners and proto-type of the church's deacons.

Tradition

This is the traditional view, as evidenced, for example, in the long entry for December 26 in the eleventh volume of Alban Butler's *Lives of the Fathers, Martyrs and Other Principal Saints* (1866). Here we read that 'St Stephen had the primacy and precedence among the deacons newly elected' and, in the words of St Augustine, that 'Stephen is named the first of the deacons, as Peter is of the apostles'.

Biblical scholars have also taken this view, perhaps most significantly the great English scholar of the nineteenth century, J. B. Lightfoot, in his famous essay on *The Christian Ministry*. This study accompanied his commentary on the Letter to the Philippians, where it was natural for Lightfoot to discuss the question of ministry at length because in Philippians 1:1 we have the earliest written evidence of the existence of officials within a Christian community named 'bishops and deacons'. In reporting them as bishops and deacons we do need to be honest and add that the Greek words for what we now call bishops and deacons occur at this place, but what precisely they stood for in the Philippian community scholars discuss. A common translation these days is 'overseers and their helpers'.

Lightfoot also notes, as many others do, that already in the second century Irenaeus identified in the seven men of Acts 6 the kind of deacons with whom he was familiar from the practice of his own church in Lyons. In addition Lightfoot reminds us that in the ancient church of Rome, out of deference to the Seven of Acts 6, deacons were never allowed to exceed the number seven and that, on the same grounds, in 315 CE the Council of Neocaesarea enacted a law limiting deacons to this number whatever the size of a city.

Tradition disputed

Such ancient authority and nineteenth-century scholarship give to the idea of an original seven deacons the look and feel of authenticity. And yet Lightfoot himself was aware that the idea of deacons so early in the church's life – and in this passage in particular – had been 'much disputed'. An historian of the modern diaconate, Jeannine E. Olson, notes how the ancient tradition has indeed lived on to the present but 'with dissenting views'. An eminent successor to Lightfoot in the study of the early church was A. M. Farrer, and he dismissed the whole idea of an original seven deacons as 'a very old error'. A prominent contemporary voice here would be that of James Monroe Barnett, a long-standing champion of the diaconate, who closes his pages on the subject with the plain statement, 'we must conclude that the Seven were *not* deacons'. This too has been the view which my own study of Acts 6 has demanded.

Accordingly, deacons of today are likely to be interested in following the line of thought which has led to this conclusion. Probably they are likely to be even more interested in how the development of ministry which Luke has sketched within the story of the very first Christian church in Jerusalem can be of value to the new deacons of today. First, however, a note of reassurance. In recent years many people have experienced moments when they have felt that certain treasured perceptions of theirs have been undermined or demolished by so-called modern biblical experts. Some perhaps have had the encouraging experience of weathering this disappointment and going on to discover within the newer biblical interpretation layers of understanding which are enlightening and enriching. In the same way I trust that the line of thought concerning the Seven which is to be sketched here is not by any means detrimental to the deacon's sense of identity today but will rather lead to enlarging reflections on the position of one who has been ordained to a role within the Christian community.

A broad spectrum
The reason why we must ask if these Seven were deacons can be put fairly simply even though the explanation

takes us a little further into how Luke used the Greek words which we normally associate with deacons. Probably all deacons know that what has led people to make a connection between the story in Acts 6 and the diaconate is the way Luke describes the task of the Seven as taking part in 'the daily distribution [of food]' and in 'serving at tables'. These are phrases we read in our translations, although the exact wording can differ from translation to translation.

Most deacons would also be aware that there is a word link between how Luke names these activities in Acts 6 and the title *deacon* itself. The word link is of course the Greek word *diakonia*, and Luke uses this abstract noun to designate 'the distribution [of food]' at Acts 6:1 and its corresponding verb *diakonein* to designate 'serving at tables' (6:2). In addition we need to be aware that a third instance of the words occurs in this passage when Luke uses *diakonia* to name 'the ministry of the word' (6:4) to which the Twelve decide to make an exclusive commitment.

Thus, according to our modern translations of Acts, we have the *diakon-* words identifying (a) distribution of food to needy widows; (b) the activity of serving this food at tables; and (c) the prime responsibility of the Twelve in 'the ministry' of preaching the word. This is a broad spectrum of activities to be named *diakonia*, ranging as it does from social work in something like a soup kitchen to the apostolic proclamation of the gospel. Within this scale, nonetheless, as we have noted, many have been of the opinion that the activities at the kitchen end of the spectrum were what the Twelve ordained the Seven for when they prayed over them and laid hands on them.

The outcome of such a development would go close to making this passage the defining text for the identity of deacons in the church. And this is what it became in some quarters of the historical church, especially under the teaching of John Calvin, with social work becoming the defining activity of deacons. In some sectors of the modern diaconal movement this is precisely how the modern deacon's identity has been defined, although this is not the case, officially at least, within the Roman Catholic diaconate, where the threefold role remains in place: proclamation of the word, liturgy, and works of charity.

Where is the deacon?

Thus the trend to make social work the defining role of deacons has been very strong from the time of the Reformation and on into the various modern reforms of the diaconate. A powerful influence in establishing this trend has been the passage of Acts 6:1–6. When we look closely once again, however, at what Luke is doing with this passage within the larger framework of his narrative in Acts, we have reason to pause. In looking closely we discern two features of the narrative which warn us that something could be awry in the seemingly persuasive reading that seven extra Greek men were commissioned to look after the physical needs of Greek-speaking widows who were being overlooked in the social network of the early Christian community in Jerusalem.

The first feature of the narrative is simple in the extreme. This is that Luke does not mention the word *deacon* (*diakonos* in Greek). Although the absence of the deacon's title does not of itself make an argument, it does make us ask why, if Luke was recording the founding of the order of deacons, he does not manage to call the Seven *deacons*. As a writer Luke was a skilled and sensitive user of Greek – and shows himself to be totally familiar with all that the *diakon-* words stood for in Greek language, religion and culture. In addition, his passion to show his audience the sure historical foundations of the church was matched only by his passion to present his audience with models of the church to build on for the future.

So clearly recognizable are these passions that biblical critics were once inclined to dismiss Luke's version of the growth of the Christian community as an exercise in 'early

Catholicism'. Yet nowhere in such an enthusiast for issues of church order do we come across an explicit mention of a deacon. Thus, we end up with a story about *diakon-* this and *diakon-* that, words which appear to make links with the idea of the *deacon/diakonos*, but we are left with a missing link, namely, the title *deacon/diakonos* itself.

The link to ministry

The second feature of the passage is somewhat different and consists of the way Luke's use of the *diakon-* words here links back to his uses of *diakonia* earlier in Acts. From a consideration of these links we will come to recognize that in the *diakon-* words of Acts 6 Luke might be trying to achieve an effect less specific than the establishment of the church's first deacons and more to do with the broader question of the nature of the church itself and how it is to cope with changing needs and times. It is clear, for instance, that in Acts Luke is using the *diakon-* words as code words for the kind of ministry by which the Word of God is to spread from Jerusalem. In recent years scholars have been paying closer attention to the significance of what appears at first sight to be merely a minor feature of his writing. The facts of his usage are simple to record but are impressive once we reflect on them.

Firstly, in the upper room, when Peter announces the need to fill the place in the Twelve left vacant by Judas' death, he does so in the context of the commission which Jesus laid upon these chosen ones to be 'witnesses in Jerusalem, in all Judea and Samaria, and to the ends of the earth' (Acts 1:8). Thus Peter announces the need to fill Judas' 'share in this *ministry*', in Greek 'this *diakonia*' (1:17). The word *diakonia* thus embraces the special apostolic mission to take the Word of the Lord abroad. Accordingly when the Eleven pray for enlightenment on how to fill 'the place in this *ministry* and apostleship', Luke again calls this ministry *diakonia* (1:25).

Luke does not use a *diakon-* word again until Acts 6:1, where he refers to 'the daily *ministry/diakonia*' (which we have already met in the phrase of the modern translation, 'daily distribution [of food]'). Then, in the same part of the story, again as already seen, the Twelve rededicate themselves to their original commission of 'the ministry/*diakonia* of the word' (6:4). Luke then closes the scene of the Seven with the tell-tale phrase, 'the word of God continued to spread' (6:7).

With these touches Luke keeps us in mind of his major theme as he moves into the great preaching event in the brief career of Stephen, one of the Seven (7:2–53). With Stephen's death immediately following, the theme of the progress of the Word re-emerges in the account of another member of the Seven, Philip, engaging in a mission to Samaria; Samaria is the first station outside Jerusalem and Judea according to the stages of the Lord's programme outlined by Luke (1:8). This mission leaves Philip poised at Caesarea, the port leading to Rome (8:4–14; 26–40), which is Luke's ultimate objective in the trajectory of the Word.

With that great objective of the Lord's programme almost in sight, it is not surprising that Luke next introduces us to Paul, the one whom the Lord called 'an instrument whom I have chosen to bring my name before Gentiles and kings' (9:15). The Lord was to hustle Paul along the road because, as the Lord said to him, 'you must bear witness also in Rome' (23:11). Having glimpsed this grand geographical and missionary framework, we have no difficulty recognizing that Luke is intending to make Paul an integral part of the master plan which Luke identified in chapter 1 as 'this ministry/*diakonia* and apostleship' (1:25) and by which the witness was to reach from Jerusalem to the ends of the earth.

Not surprisingly, therefore, when Paul completes his third heroic tour of Asia and is making his way back to the church in Jerusalem, he leaves the following missionary dedication ringing in the ears of the elders of Ephesus (20:24):

I do not count my life of any value to myself, if only I may finish my course and the ministry/*diakonia* that I received from the Lord Jesus, to testify to the good news of God's grace.

The striking element here is the reappearance of the ministerial code-word *diakonia*. The word is clearly identifying the strenuous mission which Paul had undertaken at the behest of his Lord and by which the Word of God's grace has been reaching abroad. Any doubt as to the significance of this wordplay of *diakonia* across Luke's narrative of the spread of the Word of God dissipates in the next and last use of the word in Luke. This is when Paul has completed the transit from Ephesus to the mother church in Jerusalem. There, in the presence of James, the leader, and of all the elders of the church, Paul makes a report of what 'God had done among the Gentiles through his ministry/ *diakonia*' (21:19).

At the heart of Luke's history of the Christian mission, then, we have the word *diakonia* marking the major stages of its progress. In this narrative the term *diakonia* marks the beginning of the Twelve's mission (1:17,25), it is there at the peak of their mission to Jerusalem (6:4), it is there to mark Paul's inclusion in the mission (20:24), and it is there when Paul completes his part of it (21:19).

Impact of the Word

In the light of this striking pattern of usage, the question arises, therefore, what is the relevance to this same grand story of the one other unexplained instance of the code-word at the beginning of the narrative of the Seven (6:1). If we are persuaded that Luke has worked the code word into his long narrative for the purpose of indicating how he understands the complementary nature of the roles of the major evangelizers, the Twelve and Paul, we perhaps need to reconsider whether 'distribution [of food]' does justice to the idea Luke had in mind for the one remaining instance of the word in the context of the Seven (6:1).

An important part of this reconsideration is to look at Luke's narrative between Acts 1:6 and 6:1 from another perspective. We have been looking at it from the perspective of the mission to spread the Word. We will look at it now from the perspective of the effects which the Word was producing among the believers within the first church in Jerusalem. From this perspective we see that Luke is emphasizing the changes brought about in the lives of believers by the impact of the Word. As with the story of the spread of the Word to Rome, so in this narrative Luke presents his viewpoint with dramatic emphasis, even though it is intermingled in these chapters with the higher drama of the proclamation of the Word in the hostile environment of the Temple.

The dimension of difficulty and danger which relations with the institution of the Temple introduce into the mission gives a sharp definition to the picture of the community of believers which is continuously building under the lively power of the Word. Luke's sketches of the affairs of the community under these challenging conditions are familiar. The believers are 'constantly devoting themselves to prayer, together with certain women' (1:14); they are 'all together in one place' when invested with the power of the Spirit (2:1); they 'devoted themselves to the apostles' teaching and fellowship, to the breaking of bread and the prayers' (2:42); they 'were together and had all things in common ...' (2:44–7); they 'were of one heart and soul, and no one claimed private ownership of any possessions, but everything they owned was held in common' (4:32); 'there was not a needy person among them ...' (4:34).

So sacred is this bond between them, welded by the power of the Word, that they sold their possessions, 'laid the proceeds at the apostles' feet, and it was distributed to each as any had need' (4:34–5). So sacred is the bond that when it is momentarily broken by Ananias and Sapphira, who keep some of the proceeds, the very life of the pair drains away from them (5:1–11). It is as if the pair had stepped outside the life-giving environment of the community.

Throughout all this building of community the intensive campaign of the mission proceeded in the temple, led intrepidly by Peter and John. Flogged and forbidden to 'speak in the name of Jesus' (5:40), they merely rejoiced to 'suffer dishonour for the sake of the name' (5:41). At this dramatic point Luke brings to an end his account of the mission to Jerusalem on the part of the Twelve with the statement: 'And every day in the temple and at home they did not cease to teach and proclaim Jesus as the Messiah.' (5:42)

Good listeners

In our New Testaments that statement about proclaiming Jesus marks the end of chapter 5. This division of chapters tends to obscure for us the connection with what immediately follows at the opening of chapter 6. (The chapter divisions were added centuries later.) Luke proceeds with a phrase which is a typical opener to a new development in the narrative: 'In those days ...' It is as if Luke is writing, 'In the course of these activities ...' Indicating as much, Luke's next phrase is, 'with the expansion in the number of disciples'. And then we have the mention of the complaint from the Hellenists, who were Greek-speaking Jews living in or visiting Jerusalem, that 'their widows were being neglected in the daily *diakonia*' (6:1).

What is a reader to make of this? More pertinently, perhaps, what is an audience – for Luke's was largely an aural culture – to make of this, particularly listeners who were attuned to the Greek language and, like Luke, to the innuendoes created in his narrative by the prior uses of *diakonia* (1:17,25). Indeed one is justified in adding that the audience was attuned also to Luke's subsequent uses of *diakonia* in the later narrative, because the audience used this story more than just once and was familiar with its development.

In addition to their awareness of Luke's own usage, the

ancient audience would also certainly relate *diakonia* in this narrative to other kinds of Greek historical and romantic narrative where *diakonia* held a well known and easily recognizable place as a word designating sacred commissions of one kind or another. We can thus be confident that Luke was intending to point the audience in this direction by the sheer force of the narrative's momentum.

In other words, the ancient audience would understand at 6:1 that the Greek-speaking widows were being overlooked in the daily preaching of the Word. This is to be understood by us in the sense that, as speakers of Greek and, further, as widows without the same freedom as Jewish women to take part in the kind of public life that temple worship was, they were neither free to attend the large gatherings in the temple forecourts nor linguistically equipped to understand what these Aramaic preachers were saying when they returned from the temple to speak in the intimacy of the household (5:42). Accordingly, the Hellenists' widows were in need of preachers who could teach them in Greek, and preferably at home when Greek-speakers came together at their tables (6:2).

A new group of preachers

Could the ancient audience have understood the scene of 6:1 in any other way? Could it really have envisaged Luke meaning that the widows were being neglected day by day in 'the distribution [of food]' (6:1)? In Luke's outline of the bonding of the community of believers, was not his last story the account of how life drained from Ananias and Sapphira for breaking that bond, and was not his last comment at the end of that story about 'the great fear [that] seized the whole church' (5:11) at the very thought that the bond could come under threat?

It would seem to be impossible that at 6:1 the skilled author Luke could be introducing a situation where the most vulnerable members of the adult society, namely the foreign widows, should be exposed to neglect. His whole effort has rather been to establish that alongside the coura-

geous work of proclamation in Jerusalem – the *'diakonia
and apostleship'* received from the Lord (1:25) – another
work has been proceeding by which the intimate community of believers has been so nurtured that 'there was not
a needy person among them' (4:34).

What does this make of the Seven? It makes of the Seven
a new group of preachers, directed at first to the needs of
the Hellenists – note how happily the story ends at 6:7: 'the
word of God continued to spread; the number of disciples
increased greatly in Jerusalem …' – and then, after the
death of Stephen in Jerusalem, to the wide worlds beyond,
as begun in Philip's mission (8:5). Indeed the only other
time we hear of Philip he is called simply 'the evangelist,
one of the seven' (21:8).

Taking the liberty of paraphrase, and including a
number of explanatory phrases, we might reread Luke's
account of the Seven in the following way:

> The Greek-speaking members of the community
> complained against those who spoke Aramaic that their
> housebound widows were being overlooked in the
> great preaching (*diakonia*) that was going on day by day
> in the environs of the Temple. So the Twelve summoned
> the whole complement of the disciples and said: 'We
> cannot possibly break off our public proclamation
> before the huge crowds in the Temple to carry out a
> ministry (*diakonein*) in the households of these Greek-
> speaking widows. Brothers, you will have to choose
> seven men from your own ethnic group who are fully
> respected, empowered by the Spirit, and equipped for
> the task. We will then appoint them to the role that
> needs to be filled. That will mean that the Twelve can
> get on with attending to worship in the Temple and to
> our apostolic ministry (*diakonia*) of proclaiming the
> Word there.

Feed the hungry

Matthew 25:44 *'Lord, when did we see you hungry and not serve you?'*
The New Testament provides strong indications that support of the needy is an activity giving meaning to life within Christian communities. Love of neighbour gives meaning both to the community which gives and to the community which receives. We will see this principle operating in accounts of relations between communities in Antioch and Jerusalem in Acts and again between the needy community of Jerusalem and the communities founded by Paul in Asia and Greece. These communal responses to need are of particular interest to deacons. But support of the needy is also a responsibility of the individual, and the call of the gospel is heard most clearly there. Thus we will look here at one story in the gospel of special interest to deacons to see whether deacons have a special claim to it or whether the story lays a claim on every Christian. The story is about the king judging the nations in Matthew 25.

Frustrations
Pursuing our lives within a culture which exalts the individual, we too easily lose sight of communal connections. Perhaps it would be fairer to say that we have connections with so many sub-communities that we draw more resolutely on our individual resources to hold the threads of life in tension and give it a necessary sense of purpose. The multi-directional focuses in our lives tend to deprive us of a sense of the communal dimension of the works of charity. This is not to say that corporate works of charity by institutions like the Red Cross and Amnesty International leave us unaware of the importance and effectiveness of strategic action. The situation for the member of a Christian congregation today is rather that the individual feels Christian charity is more than support of corporate projects. The individual retains a strong personal feeling

of the burden of need, and of frustration about how much an individual can do to meet need or create situations that prevent need. Not far away is the feeling of guilt at seeming to achieve or even to attempt so little.

These feelings are intensified for many because of the constant impact made on them by fleeting daily experiences like an unexpected encounter in a shopping centre with someone affected by drugs, by regular front page stories of loss and grief, and, at the end of a day's work, by a phone call soliciting financial support just when we are being confronted on television by distressing images and on-the-spot reporting from a disaster area. In addition are the regular mail drops, the advertisements and inserts for appeals in newspapers and journals, and finally the call from a priest at the end of a Sunday liturgy for a special collection. Strangely, this last can appear somehow far removed from the real needs of the world. It can also appear to have only a tenuous or at least artificial link with what the liturgical gathering has been about.

The persistent call

Such experiences do not make it any easier for Christians to know what to make of probably the most familiar saying of the gospel – although it is really a word of the Torah – 'Love your neighbour as yourself' (Leviticus 19:18; Luke 10:27). Their hesitations and confusion arise not only because they might not be sure what love means in regard to a neighbour – let alone to an enemy, to whom Jesus also extends love (Matthew 5:44) – but also because the call for response to need today is put mostly in money terms. Most Christians of course, like most non-Christians, are themselves living below or on the borderline of financial security and manage their affairs with difficulty. But the sense of individual personal responsibility is all the more persistent because of the sheer success of two stories which the gospels report of Jesus.

Both of these stories are parables, and one of them challenges the story of the two lost sons in Luke 15 as the most famous story attributed to Jesus. It is the story of the Good Samaritan in Luke 10. Its impact is all the stronger because Jesus tells it for the specific purpose of answering the teacher's question, 'Who is my neighbour?' Today's audience ends up being confronted with images of an individual person performing a range of challenging, expensive, and time-consuming tasks almost certainly beyond the means and competence of individuals in our kind of society.

The call of the gospel is nonetheless unmistakable, and over the comparatively short history of the modern diaconate this call has been the single most influential factor in its development. Extending love to the neighbour remains critical to deacons' perception of their place in the church. As is clear from earlier comments, the modern diaconal movement began precisely for the purpose of providing loving service to the needy, and from its earliest years leaders of the movement cultivated an understanding that the title 'deacon' was chosen by the earliest Christians to express a relationship of loving service to those in need. The order of the diaconate is itself designated *diakonia* in Greek, and in several modern European languages this word has become the standard expression for works of service and love in the name of the church.

A dramatic word

Given such links between the title which deacons have and the task which they have set themselves in today's church, the story in Matthew 25 of the king judging the nations has a special appeal. As deacons are aware, the appeal lies largely in the way the drama reaches its peak the moment a *diakon-* word is used in the narrative. We see it in the following extract, where the condemned are making their futile appeal to the king.

> 'Lord, when did we see you hungry or thirsty or a stranger or naked or ill or in prison and did not *serve* (*diakon-*) you?'

Naturally deacons immediately take note of this moment in the story because they have almost certainly come to understand this as the moment when people are condemned for not having performed the kind of loving service known as *diakonia*. Given this expectation of the story's meaning among deacons, the story has become theirs in a way few other Christians would dare to claim for themselves because the story speaks of what deacons are trying to do with their whole lives. Even if, as we will now see, a clearer understanding of the *diakon-* words requires that we locate the drama of the final scene in a different interplay, the story will always carry a special values for deacons.

Two clues

There are two clues to understanding how the story is working at this moment in the lives of one tragic group of its characters. One clue is in the structure of the story to this point, and the other is in understanding why the narrator draws on the service/*diakon-* word at the same point. Taking the *diakon-* word first, we recall that in the Son of Man's teaching about discipleship in Mark 10:42–5 Jesus developed the teaching on the basis of comparing life within the discipleship with life in the grand houses. In the grand houses of those governing the nations – that is, within the official establishments of Roman Prefects like Pontius Pilate in Caesarea – the persons who had absolutely no share in the exercise of the power by which the Prefect maintained the Emperor Tiberius' absolute control of the Jewish people were the many 'attendants' (*diakonoi*) and 'slaves' (*douloi*) who made life comfortable for the Prefect and his retinue of family, friends, officials and hangers-on.

Now while the 'attendants' would have been slaves, they are called *diakonoi* because of their particular responsibility in the area of the personal needs of the leading figures in such establishments and, as well, in seeing that everything was in order for the efficient running of daily affairs in these establishments. One could compare differences of status between mere household slaves and such attendants with the differences in the grander households of nineteenth-century London between the butler or valet and a kitchenhand. Ancient accounts of affairs in great houses and royal palaces present a clear picture of such *diakonoi*.

The setting of this story is, of course, in a royal court of the most awful grandeur because it opens with an image of the powerful figure from the vision in the Book of Daniel coming 'in glory' and sitting on 'his glorious throne' (Matthew 25:31) This figure is of course Daniel's 'one like a son of man' (Daniel 7:13). In that vision, when the Ancient of Days sat in judgement upon all the empires of the world, he gave dominion and judgement over all of them to 'one like a son of man' whose honours ranked above anything known upon earth. Such is 'the glory' which the opening of the story is referring to. As the story develops the storyteller keeps the audience keenly aware of the status of this dominant figure, henceforth identified as 'the king'. And the high reward for those in whose favour he judges is nothing less than to 'inherit the kingdom that has been prepared' for them.

A kingdom of people

The king's judgement of the group assembled at his right hand itemizes the deeds these people have performed, all of them works of assistance to someone in need: 'you gave me something to eat ...; you gave me a drink ...; you took me in ...; you clothed me ...; you looked after me ...; you visited me ...' The striking thing about this judgement is that the king assesses as having been done to himself those actions which these people have performed to strangers and others in need whom they have met. Clearly the king's kingdom is his people, not just a territory, and all people are to recognize the royal bond uniting them to one another and, together, to the king.

The way the storyteller makes it emphatically clear that

the unifying bond within the kingdom is made up of the myriad threads of helping actions is by repeating the list of helping actions three more times. Thus, in response to the king's favourable judgement of them, the people on the king's right-hand side put a series of questions to him: 'When … did we feed you or give you a drink? When … did we take you in or clothe you? When … did we come to you?' The list appears again when the king gives unfavourable judgement on the people on his left-hand side: 'you did not give me anything to eat… ; you did not give me a drink… ; you did not take me in… ; you did not clothe me… ; you did not take care of me'. The impact of such charges are, of course, devastating. These people have already known before hearing the detailed list that they are to be consigned to 'the everlasting fire prepared for the devil and his messengers'.

In a summary fashion

Just as the story contains three detailed lists of the works required of his people by the king, so there are also three summary references to the list of the works. The first is when the king replies to the astonished query from the people on his right-hand side as to when they had acted so helpfully to the person of the king. The king replies in a summary fashion, 'Whenever *you did these things to* one of these most marginalized of my family members *you did it to me*'. Similarly in his reply to the query from the condemned group on his left: 'As often as *you did not do these things to* one of these most marginalized people, *you did not do them to* me'. In other words, on two occasions the king sums up the whole list of helpful actions of feeding, giving a drink, offering shelter, providing clothes, taking care and visiting in the plain words, '*did*' or '*did not do*' (*epoiēsate*).

   In the third summary statement, however, this summary word suddenly changes. In the desperate appeal of the condemned people they put the following question to the king: 'Lord, when did we see you hungry or thirsty

or a stranger or naked or sick or in gaol and not *serve* you?'
The summary word changes from 'doing things for you' to
'serving you', and the Greek word here is the *diakon-* verb
for *serving a royal person*. As such, the word has a significant role in the unfolding of what is happening at this
stage of narrative.

By this stage of the story, by force of the detailed repeti-
tions, the audience is thoroughly aware of what the
teacher is teaching. This is, that helping people in their
specific needs is what makes a person a member of the
king's household. The people who were favourably
judged had been as unaware of this as the people who
were condemned. They had to have explained to them
how the king required his subjects to live in relation to
each other. Those who have been condemned, however,
are not open to any such explanation because the terms of
their question to the king show that their lives are focused
exclusively on the royal person and that they are totally
unaware that other people matter. The clear indication
that they think the only value in life is to attend to the
royal person without regard to his 'family members' is
their appeal to their royal service or *diakonia.*

Grounds for condemnation

Thus, in this story, far from being a word relating to
helping people in need, the *diakon-* word used by the
condemned people is expressing their deafness to the call
of the kingdom for all its brothers and sisters to help one
another cope with life's difficulties. The word is not a
Christian code word for lowly and loving help, but is
acting rather as a sign that the condemned have not yet
begun to think of the nature of their place and responsibilities in the household of the king. It is a sign that they
are locked in to a self-contained world. Inside their world
they think only of the master and of rewards that may
come to them from ignoring all other people in order to
anticipate the master's own indulgent desires.

From the church in Antioch to the church in Jerusalem

Acts 11:29 *'They decided to send a delegation to the members living in Jerusalem'*
If a close examination of language in the parable of the judging of the nations shows that *diakon-* is not there a code-word for the kind of loving service which deacons cherish as the special mark of their role in the church, they are still to read in this story the profound challenge which it puts before them as before all Christians. The story loses nothing of its special relevance to the role of deacons in the church, and indeed continues to display how important it is for service to the needy to be modelled from within the heart of the church.

From the heart of the church

A similar message is to be taken from those other passages in the New Testament which use *diakon-* words in the reporting of delegations which early churches sent to the mother church of Jerusalem in order to alleviate its needs in times of distress. Unfortunately our bible translations and bible dictionaries show little sensitivity to the way the language is working in these reports. Almost uniformly they present *diakon-* as expressing ideas connected with help for those in need. The reports are nonetheless particularly clear expressions of how ancient Greeks commonly used the *diakon-* words in accounts of delivering messages.

The simplest passage to illustrate this in the New Testament is one in the Acts of the Apostles. Typically the writer is Luke, whose sensitivity to *diakon-* words we have noted in discussing Jesus' discourse at the Passover meal and the commissioning of the Seven in Acts 6. In Acts 11:27–30 Luke tells how the church of Antioch responded to a forecast of impending famine by organizing to send assistance to the church in Jerusalem. After an interlude in the narrative, Luke records the conclusion of the episode at 12:25.

The scene is simply set. On hearing the prophetic warning of famine, the disciples in Antioch determine that each member of the community should contribute to the aid package. They choose two members of their community, Barnabas and Paul, to deliver their contribution. Such pairing of delegates was conventional in the Hellenistic world.

In addition to the pairing, several other indications in the account point to the formal character of the undertaking. Barnabas and Paul will be presenting the community's contribution to the leaders of the church in Jerusalem ('the elders'), and the community formally despatches (11:30, *aposteilantes*) them. This fits with the phrase from the preceding verse that the community had formally determined (*hōrisan*) to undertake the task.

On a mission

The narrative identifies the task as sending some of their members 'upon a mission' to Judea. The Greek for this is *eis diakonian*. The idea of mission at this point of the narrative is never picked up in translations in English, although the phrase is a standard expression of this sense in ancient Greek. Strangely, what we do notice in some English and other translations – the new Swedish *Bibel 2000* is an example – is that when the same word *diakonia* recurs at the conclusion of the episode it appears in the sense of 'mission'. Thus, the RSV: 'when they had completed their mission' (12:25). This should be the sense of the word also at 11:29: 'without exception the community of disciples determined to send *representatives on a mission* to the brothers and sisters living in Judea'.

Almost universally, however, at 11:29 bibles translate *diakonia* as 'aid', 'relief', 'help'. In doing this translators are making an error, it is true, and those who go on to translate *diakonia* at 11:29 as 'mission' are being inconsistent as well, but they are also contributing significantly to fixing the idea that *diakonia* is a Christian expression for help to the needy.

That idea of helping should never have been introduced into this narrative. We should read the story as Luke intended it to be read. As such, it is a brief but studied statement of the sense of interdependence between communities which marks so many reports from early Christian times. We shall see more elaborate play upon this sense in accounts of similar situations in Paul's letters.

As Luke's passage now stands, however, it is a signal incident illustrating the importance he attached to the idea of mutual obligations linking Christian communities. The challenge which Matthew's parable of the judgement of the nations throws out to every individual Christian (Matthew 25:31–46) also becomes, on Luke's view, a challenge to each church to be seen to be acting corporately in works of love. But the word *diakonia* was never the expression of that love.

From the churches in Asia to the church in Jerusalem

Romans 15:25 *'I am on my way to Jerusalem on a mission from the saints.'*
In several other places in the New Testament, translations of recent decades have been distorting our understanding of activities in the first Christian communities. These activities are similar to that involved in the mission from Antioch to Jerusalem reported by Luke in Acts 11:27–30. As noted there, the misrepresentation of such missions is unfortunate not only because the Bible is being translated incorrectly but also because today's Christian communities are being deprived of an opportunity to reflect on a remarkable way by which the first churches sought to express communion among themselves. As also noted in regard to the delegation in Acts 11, when modern translators of the Bible lead us to understand the *diakon-* words in these accounts as expressions of loving help, they are strongly reinforcing the modern misconception that

diakonia in the church, and in particular the *diakonia* of deacons, is essentially a service of loving care.

In the years – indeed in the centuries – before English terms from the *ministry* group were replaced as translations of the *diakon-* words by terms from the *service* group, this problem did not arise nearly so easily. One sees this, for example, when the explanatory note to Romans 15:25 in the Geneva Bible of 1602 explains 'to minister unto the Saints' as '*Doing his duty for the Saints* ... '. This was because the term *ministry* or *administer* did not carry suggestions about loving service which words of the *service* group could readily suggest. At the same time, however, words of the *ministry* group were not always adequate to express ideas relating to delegations.

Discrepancies

We can observe a wide discrepancy between ways translations present Paul's discussion of the mission to Jerusalem. His writings in 2 Corinthians 8–9, which are two separate interventions on the matter, and in Romans 15, show how deeply he involved himself in this mission. Paul has become aware that the church in Jerusalem is experiencing financial difficulties. In wishing to relieve some of its problems, he conceived the idea of the churches that he had established in Asia Minor and Greece organizing a collection of money.

In the course of making arrangements for this, Paul has also perceived a political opportunity. Since the church in Jerusalem retained its strong Jewish tradition, there were those in its community who were deeply suspicious of what they had learnt of churches among the Greeks and other Gentiles. This would have been especially so as most of the Judean Christians were in fact observant Jews. Since, however, Paul was preparing to return to Jerusalem to report on the condition of the mainly Gentile churches in the territories of his mission, he grasped the advantage offered by this visit of presenting to the leaders in Jerusalem substantial financial assistance.

Paul's thinking here was not purely political. It was also typical of the deeply theological attitude he brought to all his dealings in matters of the churches. The gift from the churches would not simply be an act of charity. Much more than that, it would be a demonstration to the church leaders in Jerusalem that Gentiles in distant lands were responding to the Spirit of God in ways which demonstrated the authentic character of their churches. To help ensure that the gift would be seen in this light, Paul took great care to make it appear that the gift was of the churches' own making and was not simply something which he had organized. His way of doing this was to have delegates from various communities accompany the gift to Jerusalem. For himself, he was part of the delegation and, as such, would be acting on behalf of the churches. It was for this reason that in the surviving correspondence relating to the delegation we see Paul expressing himself in terms of *diakonia*. In this he was using language in exactly the same way as we have seen Luke using it in reporting on a delegation from the church in Antioch to the church in Jerusalem.

If we compare the two ways of representing the *diakon*-words in English, we at once see a difference in how we understand the objective behind the collection. In order to restrict the focus to this issue, in the following table the full text of Paul's discussion is reduced to relevant abstracts. The abstract in (a) draws on RSV for the translation of phrases containing a *diakon*- word. Translation (b) is my own.

(a) The underlined phrases from 2 Corinthians 8:4,19,20; 9:1,12,13; Romans 15:25,31 contain a *diakon*- word, which RSV translates without reflecting any sense of delegation.	(b) The underlined phrases from 2 Corinthians 8:4,19,20; 9:1,12,13; Romans 15:25,31 translate a *diakon*- word to convey the required sense of delegation.

The Macedonian churches have begged me most earnestly to take part with us in *the relief of* the saints.	The Macedonian churches have begged me most earnestly to take part with us in *the sacred mission to* the saints.
A brother has been appointed by the churches to travel with us in this gracious work *which we are carrying on* for the glory of the Lord.	A brother has been appointed by the churches to travel with us *as we bear* this gift *under mandate* for the glory of the Lord.
We intend that no one should blame us about this liberal gift *which we are administering.*	We intend that no one should blame us about this generous undertaking *that we have been commissioned to carry out.*
It is superfluous to write to you about *the offering for* the saints.	It is superfluous to write to you about *the sacred mission to* the saints.
The *rendering* of this service supplies the needs of the saints.	*Carrying out the sacred mandate* of this public undertaking supplies the needs of the saints.

Under the test of _this service_ they will glorify God.	In the public reception accorded to _this sacred mission_ they will glorify God.
At present I am going to Jerusalem _with aid for_ the saints.	At present I am going to Jerusalem _on a mission from_ the saints.
Pray that _my service for_ Jerusalem may be acceptable.	Pray that _my sacred mission to_ Jerusalem may be acceptable.

The language of saints

In the translation (a) we have _diakon-_ translated by RSV as _relief, offering, service, aid._ Each of these words could suggest to readers that _diakon-_ words were especially favoured by early Christians because they expressed ideas relating to helping. On the other hand in the same translation other instances of _diakon-_ words appear as _carrying on_ (in the sense of _carrying out_), _administering_ (the same idea as the preceding), and _rendering_ (also the same). The differences between these two sets of ideas – one centring on _helping_, the other on _managing_ – are striking. In fact they suggest rather strongly that in these passages the translators were struggling to come to grips with just how Paul was using the _diakon-_ words.

In hitting on the idea of management here and there, however, the translators were coming quite close to the central idea which Paul was concerned to express in all instances of the _diakon-_ words in these passages. Thus translation (b) uniformly reflects that central idea. Paul is using _diakon-_ words because they accurately convey the idea that in taking a collection of money from churches in

Asia to the church in Jerusalem he is only acting under the mandate of the Asian churches. In adopting these expressions Paul was not using or inventing an idiom peculiar to early Christians but simply following standard conventions of the Greek language. What is helpful to Paul in this convention, however, is that it allows him to give expression to the notion that the delegation was a sacred task. At no stage in the history of the ancient Greek language were the *diakon-* words part of diplomatic language, but on the other hand they were very much part of religious discourse. And this is why the words suggested themselves to Paul in the course of discussing relations between one group of 'saints' and another. The whole discussion in fact is cast in words particularly rich in religious connotation, and this style of language says much to us of the sense of church which these people had. They had a lively understanding of church as a gathering of those brought together in the Spirit.

Phoebe and other delegates of the churches

Romans 16:1 *'I commend to you our sister Phoebe, who is a delegate of the church in Cenchreae.'*
Of immediate interest to deacons, especially women deacons, is the widespread notion that the woman heading the extraordinary list of Christians in chapter 16 of Paul's letter to the church in Rome is a deacon. The woman is Phoebe, the first among many men and women to whom Paul pays tribute for the various ways they were contributing to the Christian mission and to life in the churches.

Translations in many modern languages lead us to understand that the title given to her by Paul (*diakonos*) identifies her as a deacon. In English she is sometimes presented as a deaconess, although in what sense this could be is next to impossible to determine. Even to name her a deacon raises awkward questions because the term 'deacon' implies that church order of a much later period was already somehow in place in Rome around 50 CE. On the other hand, quite commonly Phoebe is simply called a servant of the community at Cenchreae, this being the port of Corinth and the home of the church to which she belonged.

The idea of Phoebe offering services to her community seems to be supported by the other information which Paul supplies about her. This is that she has been a generous supporter of many people, including Paul himself. The additional word Paul uses here (*prostatis*/patron) would suggest that Phoebe was in a position to provide support by reason both of her means and of her social standing.

An important visitor

Closer examination of the setting suggests, however, that we can be more precise about the kind of *diakonos* this woman was. Paul mentions Phoebe first in his interesting list because he wants to introduce her to the various communities in Rome. By contrast, the other 26 people named in the list are already resident in Rome, and Paul is extending to them warm greetings from himself and from 'all the churches of Christ' (Romans 16:16).

From brief comments about people on the list we find that Paul's interest centres entirely on what these individuals have contributed to the promotion of the mission or to support of their community. Some of the people have been his own collaborators, one is a relative, 9 of 27 are women, including Tryphaena and Tryphosa, a pair of women who have joined forces in working for the gospel. Most prominent and most lavishly praised are the wife and husband team Prisca and Aquila (verses 3–5). Another possibly married couple is Andronicus and Junia, the latter name long disguised in Bibles as that of a man (Junias instead of Junia). The reason for this ancient misrepresentation appears to be that Paul had honoured her and Andronicus as 'prominent among the apostles' (verse 7), a ranking considered impossible for a woman.

What these and other details in the list are telling us is that in concluding his letter to the Romans in this way, and in keen anticipation of his own first visit to them (Romans 15:22–24), Paul is focusing strongly on keeping them aware of the ongoing tasks of consolidating the churches and expanding the mission of the gospel. In chapter 15 he has made clear his own commitment to move on to Spain for the first time after the completion of the delegation to Jerusalem that we considered in the preceding section.

Against this background the figure of Phoebe the *diakonos* stands in a different light. Neither a deacon nor just a helper of her own community, as *diakonos* she is placed by Paul in a role like that which he filled during his delegation from Asia to Jerusalem. In the case of his own delegation, in which he was actually engaged at the very time of writing, Paul was acting under the mandate of the Asian churches. In Phoebe's case, he presents her to the Roman communities as 'a delegate (*diakonos*) of the church in Cenchreae'. Being the woman of standing that she was – *prostatis* is the significant term Paul used, 'benefactor' or 'patron', but carrying considerable prestige in a culture where public honour was hard won but highly praised – the community had selected her to conduct business of a kind unknown to us in Rome on their behalf. Given Paul's preoccupations with the gospel, it would be very difficult to think of this business having to do with anything other than the gospel. Indeed, the very choice of title certainly indicates that the woman is acting in some religious capacity, because that is the character of the title and the nature of the context in which she appears.

So richly suggestive is this context that attractive surmises have in fact been made that, at Paul's instigation, the community of Cenchreae had sent Phoebe to Rome so that she might use her influence with Roman civil authorities to facilitate Paul's access to Spain. Some task of that calibre would be appropriate for a woman so highly honoured here, so earnestly commended to a vibrant

Christian community, and so singularly identified as a delegate.

References to delegations within other churches and in different circumstances are scattered through the early Christian literature. It is to another of these that Paul refers in his statement about the household of Stephanas. Members of the household – Stephanas himself, Fortunatus and Achaicus – made themselves available for a journey from Corinth to Ephesus on business to do with their church and Paul: 'You know that the household of Stephanas has made themselves available for a delegation on behalf of the saints' (1 Corinthians 16:15).

The famous slave Onesimus, whom Paul mentions in his letter to Philemon and about whom so much has been written in recent scholarship, is usually presented in translations and in commentaries upon the text as waiting on Paul's personal needs; we are actually to understand that Paul himself was wanting to engage him for the purpose of liaising with some of his clientele during the period of Paul's imprisonment (Philemon 13). Others filling similar roles are Epaphras (Colossians 1:7), Tychicus (Colossians 4:7–9; Ephesians 6:21), and the two companions of Paul's journeying mentioned by Luke in Acts 19:22, Timothy and Erastus.

That this style of reporting interchanges between churches by way of *diakon-* remains conventional we see in some letters of Ignatius of Antioch. In his writings the sense of the common religious bond drawing communities together is particularly strong. An illustration would be the string of godly terms he invokes in regard to a delegation to Antioch organized by Polycarp (Polycarp 7:2–3). Here we meet the odd word, 'God's runner' (*theodromos*), which sums up the early Christian perception of the hidden but godly links between all those who believe and experience the benevolence of God. The words *diakonos* and *diakonia* expressed exactly the same connections, as we can see in his letter to the Philadelphians (10:1–2).

Such expressions are interesting because they crop up in

a writer who has much to say about deacons. Yet the expressions remain distinguishable from deacon language. As applied to deacons on representative missions, as in the cases of Burrhus, who was a deacon, and the pair of delegates Philo, another deacon, and Rheus, we have no trouble distinguishing which role Ignatius is referring to when he speaks of them as 'God's envoys/*diakonoi*' (*Smyrnaeans* 10:1) involved in 'God's mission/*diakonia*' (12:1).

If evidence of such representative activity by deacons on behalf of their churches prompts reflection on the possible value of the practice for a church today, we ought also to bear in mind the stronger evidence that membership of such delegations was normally made up of a number of people. This was in line not only with Jewish custom in their frequent exchanges of visits between communities, but also with civic and business deputations. At the same time the fact that early Christians could use a deacon in this capacity reflects their awareness of the deacon as a person at the heart of their community and well equipped to represent its faith and love.

Heaven's gift

From some time late in the first century we have the Letter to the Ephesians. The New Testament ascribes this interesting document to Paul, but only a minority of scholars would be confident of such a claim. Most would rather ascribe the document to a close student of Paul who brings together much of that early teacher's thinking about the work of Christ and the nature of the church. This general character of the letter suggests that it was to be delivered to numerous churches instead of to a particular church or to an individual like Paul's authentic letters. Perhaps the fact that the name of Ephesus is missing from the line of address in the oldest and best of the Greek manuscripts (Ephesians 1:1) reflects the author's intention of addressing as broad an audience as possible. In this light we can read the letter as a kind of treatise on the nature of the church that the Lord and the apostles of old had left behind.

The letter is full of encouragement for the nurturing and growth of a Christian community, even if some of the prescriptions towards the end of the letter regarding social arrangements appear to run counter to some of Paul's own leading principles. The letter opens with a keen sense of Christians being 'blessed ... in Christ with every spiritual blessing in the heavenly places' (1:3), and proceeds to review the range of blessings of a people who are 'no longer strangers and sojourners' but are 'fellow citizens with the saints [that is, believers in the churches across the land at that time] and members of the household of God' (2:19).

Engaging mystery

Next the writer records the process which has brought his readers into an awareness of what he sees primarily as 'the mystery' (3:3). This 'mystery hidden for ages in God' (3:9) concerns 'the eternal purpose which he has realized in Christ Jesus' (3:11). As 'mystery', it was 'not known to the sons of men in other generations' (3:5) and was 'made known ... by revelation' to the writer (3:3), and not to the writer alone but also to God's 'holy apostles and prophets' (3:5), the earlier missionaries who, like Paul, had taken the Word of God from Jerusalem 'to the ends of the earth' (Acts 1:8).

Instead of simply including himself among the 'apostles', the writer reverts to the preferred term by which Paul had identified himself as a bearer of the Word of God to the Corinthians. There he and his colleague were 'ministers/*diakonoi*' (1 Corinthians 3:5), indeed, 'qualified ... ministers/*diakonoi* of a new covenant' (2 Corinthians 3:6), who were engaged in 'the ministry/*diakonia* of reconciliation' (5:18). The point of Paul's preferred language here in Ephesians was to engage Hellenistic readers in reflecting on the process to which they had been exposed in their coming to faith. The writer speaks of their 'access through ... faith' (3:12), and knows that the outcome is that they 'perceive' and attain 'insight' into the mystery (3:4). All this is a process of a growing awareness of being in connection with Christ or, as Paul's common phrase was, of being simply 'in Christ'.

On hearing of a 'minister/*diakonos*' (Ephesians 3:7) bearing 'revelation' from the other world, the Hellenistic audience at once recognized a special category of messenger. This was a messenger with the word of 'mystery', a word that entered into the consciousness of individuals and that brought its own awareness of the divine. Paul himself had been insistent on the personal dimension of this ministerial exchange. As a 'minister/*diakonos*' his first responsibility was to be 'faithful', that is, trustworthy in the performance of his mandate. Trustworthiness was the hallmark of a *diakonos*, which is why Paul adduced the evidence of the difficulties, sufferings and dangers he endured in the course of his mission (2 Corinthians 11:23–7). These were a mark of fidelity to his mandate.

For the individual recipient of the message, however, a more convincing sign of the authenticity of Paul's teaching was the inner assurance that the individual received. In appealing to this process Paul had insisted to the Corinthians that he refused 'to tamper with God's word', and in saying so he was implying that he let God's Word itself penetrate to the believer. This left him in a position where, in order to have himself acknowledged as God's messenger, he could appeal directly to 'every person's conscience' or inner awareness of God's own presence (4:2). Such an experience was itself a sign that his 'ministry/*diakonia*' had been effective and 'no fault' found with it (6:3), that is, no impediment or hindrance to the divinely-worked process. The writer of the Letter to the Ephesians is aware of this style of language, as was any literate Greek of the time. This is why he describes Paul's role in the following terms: 'Of this gospel I was made a minister/*diakonos* according to the gift of God's grace which was given me by the working of his power' (Ephesians 3:7).

Teachers' role

The writer moves on in this treatise from the stage where he has described Paul's role in enabling a church to come into being among believers, to the stage where he presents considerations of how the church actually functions. In doing so he continues to write within the category of 'ministry/*diakonia*' as a way of conveying the idea of the ongoing disbursement of heavenly mystery from on high. Thus Christ has 'ascended' in order to dispense 'to each ... according to the measure of Christ's gift' (4:7). The gift is 'the mystery' already mentioned of 'the eternal purpose which [God] has realized in Christ' (3:11). The people who take part in the 'ministry/*diakonia*' of dispensing 'his gifts' are the apostles, prophets, evangelists, pastors and teachers (4:11), that is, the various ministers/*diakonoi* both of the early years of the church (apostles, prophets) and of the more recent times (evangelists, pastors and teachers).

The purpose these teachers are to pursue across all ages of the church is expressed in the following threefold phrasing of Ephesians 4:12:

> for the equipment of the saints,
> for the work of ministry/*diakonia*,
> for building up the body of Christ.

The threefold pattern here is clearly represented in this translation from the *Revised Standard Version* edition of 1946, and faithfully represents the direction in which the writer is taking the readers. Readers are to understand that the teachers provide believers with what they require for entering into experience of the mystery; in doing so, teachers will fulfil their obligation under their mandate of ministry/*diakonia*; and this leads to building up the church.

Since 1946, however, there has been much modern disavowal of any such intention on the part of this author, and few indeed are more recent translations which provide modern readers with an opportunity to discern such an intention. The second edition itself of the *Revised*

Standard Version in 1971 changed its phrasing to the following:

> for the equipment of the saints for the work of ministry, for building up the body of Christ...

By a simple omission of a comma in the English phrasing this translation transfers 'the work of ministry' from the teachers to the saints. To transfer 'the work of ministry' in this way is to misrepresent what the author understood by 'ministry/*diakonia*' in this kind of context. It is also to introduce into what we think the church is and how we think it operates a totally different principle from the principle established by the writer. My own arguments for the correctness of the 1946 *Revised Standard Version* are included in earlier publications, and I will not take them further here.

Divine empowerments

Where modern commentators and theologians have tended to focus almost entirely on who does the ministry, the earlier commentators and theologians, like the author himself, knew who did 'the work of ministry/*diakonia*' and focused instead on what the church does in response to engaging with the mystery. What happens when mystery is engaged is that 'all' attain 'the unity of the faith and of the knowledge of the Son of God' (4:13) so that 'bodily growth' of the church will occur through the interplay of 'all' the enlightened adherents. Through such mutuality 'the whole body ... upbuilds itself in love'. (4:16).

In understanding the working principle of the church in this way, we are not only returning to a mainstream historical reading of this passage, but we are also putting ourselves in a better position to appreciate how truly the author of Ephesians was replicating the earlier thought of Paul. The same principle underlies Paul's discussion of the church's gifts in 1 Corinthians 12, but unfortunately, here again, modern commentators have devalued Paul's understanding of 'ministry/*diakonia*' to such an extent that in most writings 'ministry' now stands for little more than anything anyone does in a Christian community. Such readings cut Paul's 'ministry/*diakonia*' adrift from any notion of a sacred mandate. In Paul's own writings, however, there is no instance of this word or of its associated terms where the notion of sacred mandate is not represented. The mandate is generally his own heavenly mandate to purvey the word of God. On a number of occasions, as we have seen, the mandate is rather to carry out a specific function at the behest of a church or of the apostle, but the dimension of the sacred remained intact.

An aura of the sacred infuses Paul's whole discussion of gifts in 1 Corinthians 12. How could it be otherwise when he is reporting on the diverse riches with which the Spirit endows the church? In what he is talking about – the utterances, the healing, the interpretations – he is reporting the actual experiences of the Corinthians under the influence of the divine: the Spirit, the Lord, God (12:4–6). Great as is the diversity, all the endowments are, however, 'for the common good' (12:7), and in 'the body' – the same image for the church later used by the author of Ephesians – 'the members . . . have the same care for one another' (12:25).

Again, when the Ephesians author traced the growth-line of the church back to teaching, he was taking a lead from Paul who here names the teachers as God's primal appointments. First, second, and third are apostles, prophets, and teachers (12:28), each of these titles designating an engagement in ministry of the Word. In this way Paul was making clear that the responsibilities of teachers in the forming and maintaining of a church are foremost. The conclusion to chapter 12 leaves us in no doubt of his meaning, and I am quite sure that Paul had the same thought in mind when he opened the chapter with another threefold phrasing in which his expression 'ministries/ *diakoniai*' occurs. Thus (12:4–6):

Now there are varieties of gifts, but the same Spirit;
and there are varieties of service [ministries/*diakoniai*],
   but the same Lord;
and there are varieties of working, but it is the same
   God who inspires them all in every one.

Most commentators understand the three statements as equivalent. That is to say, 'gifts', 'service' and 'working' are seen as alternative terms for the divine empowerments within the church. Given the terms Paul uses, however, I cannot see how Paul could have had any such idea in mind. In the first place he has engaged a strongly rhetorical set of phrases for the purpose of setting up the discussion to follow. As noted, the discussion covers the wide ground of diverse endowments but issues 20 verses later in another strongly rhetorical statement about the primary function of teaching in the church. The signal that Paul had this function of teaching in mind from the very beginning of his discussion is his naming of ministries/*diakoniai* in verse 5. These are the same ministries/*diakoniai* which he forcefully drew to the Corinthians' attention in chapter 3 when defending the integrity and authenticity of Apollos and himself (1 Corinthians 3:5). In his next communications with the Corinthians Paul would very much more forcefully press the same case with the rhetorical power of the same words (2 Corinthians 3–6:13). Greek readers were totally familiar with the significance of the terms. The terms were deeply embedded in their religious consciousness as terms relating to the transfer of godly things from other realms to this.

On such grounds, argued at length and illustrated profusely elsewhere, one is compelled to read verse 5 as 'ministries/*diakoniai*' relating to the purveying of the Word of God, in other words, to 'the work of *diakonia*' which would be the primary teaching function designated by the author of Ephesians.

If this is the case, we have to reconsider the pattern underlying the threefold phrasing in verses 4–6 of 1

Corinthians 12. Instead of reading them as equivalent, we have to differentiate between them. It seems to me that scholars of a much earlier era were correct when they read verse 4 as a general proposition, namely, that there are many diverse gifts in the church; and correct also in reading verse 5 and verse 6 as identifying two different types of gifts, one being 'ministries/*diakoniai*', which were the responsibility of people like Paul and Apollos, and the other being the 'working', perhaps better translated 'energies', which expressed themselves in a diverse range of activities across the whole spectrum of the congregation.

Mandated for the common good

For an understanding of the nature and functions of the church there is much to be explored in these two approaches to what was obviously for Paul a matter of some substance. On the basis of the preferred modern reading of 1 Corinthians 12:4–6, where 'gifts', 'ministries', and 'energies' are equivalent, theologians have tried to come to terms with the implication that there would not seem to be much room left for ideas relating to office and authority in the church. Thus, in a famous essay at the dawn of modern ecclesiology, Ernst Käsemann wrote in 1949, 'all the baptized are "office-bearers"', and 'There is not even a prerogative of official proclamation, vested in some specially commissioned individual or other.'

These provocative and challenging claims have reverberated through much ecclesiology. Against them, however, we need to consider what happens to such a line of thinking when we set it against Paul's actual wordage. As rehearsed in the preceding paragraphs, the expression 'ministries/*diakoniai*' of itself incorporates 'a prerogative of official proclamation' within the functioning of the church. We know this because Paul is invoking a conventional Greek term to convey the idea that at the heart of the Christian church there exists a sacred mandate to conserve and pass on the Word of God.

What are deacons to think of such ecclesiological

juggling of words of the scriptures? In simple terms, deacons are reminded that, within a generation or so of Paul, these same words are to return to function as the designation of their own office. The designation 'minister/*diakonos*/deacon' is of itself an official indication that deacons are incorporated into the body of the church not as freelancers or volunteers or lone rangers but as mandated functionaries within their particular sphere. Paul insists that the church is rich with many gifts, but, just as individuals have the responsibility to discern the working of the Spirit within themselves – and to listen to the discernments offered by others – so each church has the responsibility to call and commission those gifted in ways that are for the common good. Numerous working parties within today's churches have struggled to come to a fuller understanding of the seemingly problematical situation of ordained deacons within a Spirit-filled and -gifted church. They have often been looking for the essential connection that constitutes deacons ecclesial persons. The problem resolves itself, however, on an understanding of what Paul and the ancients meant by ministry/ *diakonia*. We will reflect further on this in the next pages.

3

The Diakonia of Early Deacons

The previous section was called *The Diakonia of Jesus and the Early Church* because it was examining what New Testament writers meant when they applied words like *diakonia* to various facets of what they understood about Jesus and about some functions within their local churches. In other words, the passages we examined were not passages directly concerned with the way the early church understood the identity and function of those particular functionaries whom history came to call deacons in the church. In the course of these considerations, we have come to appreciate that words of the group to which *diakonia* belongs were versatile in the ways they could be applied.

Among significant findings is that the words could carry a strong religious connotation, as in the case of Jesus' own mission, of the mission of the church to spread the Word of God, of missions from one church of God to another, and of missions of individuals for their own church. But we also saw that the words could designate activities relating to serving at table, and that in this connection also *diakonia* could carry a religious connotation. The only other type of usage we encountered was in relation to providing personal services in grand houses and to persons of elevated or royal status.

In none of all this usage, however, was there any suggestion that the services were being provided out of love or benevolence. The *diakon-* words were not expressing anything about responding to a person's need. Their whole orientation, by contrast, is in the other direction, that is, back to the person who has authorized the *diakonia*. This reflects the idea of mandate lying behind all uses of the *diakon-* words. Thus it is God to whom Jesus responds in taking up his mission to lay down his life (Mark 10:45); it is the churches of Asia who mandate Paul to take a collection to Jerusalem (Romans 15:25); it is exclusively to the king that the servants think they owe their services (Matthew 25:44).

Many of the passages which we have examined are among those often most used for the purpose of illustrating the character and function of deacons. A number of the passages are actually among those which inspired the modern attempts to restore or reinvigorate the ancient order of deacons. Against this trend, however, we have been emphasizing that none of the passages is in fact directed specifically at the diaconate. On the contrary, they are all part of teaching that is directed at the church as a whole. Some of the ethical attitudes inculcated in these teachings may of course be among those which are especially important to the spiritual life and public functions of deacons, but they are not part of teaching which the early church would have understood as specifying the role of deacons. It is to passages which the early church did seem to understand as applying specifically to deacons that we turn now in this section called *The Diakonia of Early Deacons*.

Personnel of the church in Philippi

Philippians 1:1 *'To the saints in Philippi, their supervisors and attendants'*.
Much loved by many people for the religious sentiments

which it expresses, the letter to the remote community of Christians at Philippi in the north of Greece has always had a special place in Christian history and theology because the address at the beginning of the letter seems to name bishops and deacons among the recipients. The ancient Latin translations gave the impression that the translators understood Paul to be using the two terms *episkopoi* (bishops) and *diakonoi* (deacons) in this way. All classic translations in modern languages have also given this impression. The many translations of the last fifty years, however, have shown considerable hesitation about using terms like *bishops* and *deacons*, and tend to use alternatives like 'superintendents and assistants' or 'overseers and their helpers'.

A sensible approach

The main reason for the hesitation is that our titles of bishop and deacon carry very strong connotations of the complex church structures and practices which have developed over so many centuries around these offices, especially that of the bishop. Applying ideas associated with such established ecclesiastical offices to a small, newly developing group of believers in Christ around the middle of the first century is not likely to help us in the task of interpreting the document. Another reason to hesitate is that historical rivalries between traditions which emerged at the period of the Reformation, and prejudices which entered much theological debate then, have long since made it undesirable to cloud the work of interpreting ancient texts with ecclesiastical terms of later periods. While it is true that the two Greek words have been used in Greek-speaking churches throughout history for the offices of bishop and deacon, we do have to recognize that their meaning in Paul's time might best be represented by terms with less of an institutional ring about them.

Particularly awkward for understanding that bishops may have existed at this time is the fact that the letter is addressed not just to one but to several individuals called *episkopoi.* That this could mean several 'bishops' in Philippi is highly improbable because one of the reliable conclusions about the early organization of the Christian church is that there was no more than one bishop to a church. Paul does nothing to change the impression we get from 4:15 that the Philippians at this time still made up only one church. Accordingly the sensible approach to the group of people called *episkopoi* is to take a lead from the ordinary meaning of the word around this time, which is what the more recent translators have tried to do. Of course to take this approach will have an immediate effect on what we are to make of the second title, *diakonoi.* If the superintendents are not bishops, the *diakonoi* can hardly be deacons in our sense.

Linguistic evidence

While we have to take note of this situation in our attempt to construct a history of how Christian communities organized themselves in the earliest times, we are nonetheless obliged to pick up what clues we can about the association of these *diakonoi* with the *episkopoi.* For that we use evidence of a linguistic rather than a historical character, but we need not be surprised if linguistic features manage to throw at least some light into the dark nook in history that the church of Philippi remains.

All the signs from the various ways ancient Greeks used the word *diakonos* point to the fact that a *diakonos* never stands alone. This is not meant in the sense that the *diakonos* always has an accomplice who is another *diakonos* but in the sense that, wherever there is a *diakonos*, somewhere in the background is a person or group of people to whom the *diakonos* is responsible in the carrying out of a task. By definition the *diakonos* stands in relation to someone else who has mandated a task to the *diakonos.* For this linguistic reason alone it is not possible – as some writers have suggested over the years in relation to the situation in Philippi – to understand the expression *episkopoi*-and-*diakonoi* as a composite designation for just one group of people. (Some have wanted to see such a composite designation as an alternative expression for 'presbyters'.)

The intrinsic interrelatedness projected by the term *diakonos* we have seen illustrated in other situations. The situation of Phoebe as depicted at Romans 16:1 is a case in point. There we saw that by force of the title she was under an obligation to her community at Cenchreae to carry out a particular task when she reached Rome. We note, however, that she would have been called *diakonos* only for the duration of her particular mandate. In a similar way, when Paul was engaged in leading a delegation from Asia to Jerusalem with a gift for the church there, he could speak of himself as being involved in a *diakonia* (Romans 15:31) only up to the time he made his formal presentation to the elders in Jerusalem.

If those instances are referring to *diakonoi* of a kind who are involved in the accomplishment of a task or in the delivery of a gift, other *diakonoi* were also familiar to ancient Greeks. These were the *diakonoi* who performed as waiters at religious festivals that included meals. Held on an occasional basis, the festivals required much organization and the services of many functionaries, who all considered it an honour to be involved. Many of them paid for the privilege. We know some of this because of the monuments which they raised to commemorate the happy occasions and their roles in them.

The lists of officials recorded on the monuments are invariably lengthy, and the range of responsibilities carried by the officials were detailed and broad. In addition to presidents, general secretaries and their clerks, the lists include treasurers, priests, heralds, and musicians of various kinds; sometimes wine waiters are mentioned along with the cooks and *diakonoi*. That these *diakonoi* were responsible for the distribution of the meat produced by the cooks we can assume, but that their role was largely honorary is perhaps suggested by the frequent mention in the lists of young people, who we have to suspect bore the brunt of the drudgery. The *diakonoi* filled their role for a particular year and then moved up or down the list in other roles as opportunity or inclination provided. What we ought to bear in mind is that festivities such as these were still part of public life during the years of the founding of the Christian mission, and monuments recording *diakonoi* remained on public view or were still being erected as the first handfuls of Christian believers began gathering in the house of one of their number.

The use of *diakonos* as a title of one kind or another was by no means a novelty to Greek ears. Indeed, Greeks were familiar with it from other sources as well, and in particular in reference to some famed activities of gods in the popular mythologies. From time beyond memory Hermes had been honoured as the *diakonos* of Zeus to be engaged on journeys for him to the underworld or to make arrangements for a love affair on earth. The familiar rainbow was thought of as the path from heaven of the messenger Iris, named *diakonos* by the poet Aristophanes.

Contemporary with Paul

Contemporary with Paul, the narrator of a life of Aesop tells how Aesop received the gift of his artistry with words as a reward for kindness which he had shown to the messenger/*diakonos* of Isis. Paul himself, of course, laid claim to the same title in his role as apostle (1 Corinthians 3:5; 2 Corinthians 3:3; 6:4; 11:23), choosing to defend the authenticity of his mission in demonstration of this claim. We note that Paul would not have considered venturing upon such an argument unless he had been fully aware of what people knew about *diakonoi* and of the authority and religious aura with which they associated the term.

Literary and public language prior to and contemporary with Paul provides ample evidence that *diakonos* was a word to be used with respect and that indeed it could be used as a title of honour. If the designation lent dignity and authority to its bearer only so long as the mandate lasted, the mandate might nonetheless be longstanding.

This was the case with Paul in regard to his commission to spread the Word of God. He understood himself to be committed for life to the task or *diakonia* that he had received from the Lord.

Among holy ones

All of these linguistic characteristics add value to the title Paul addressed to some individuals in Philippi. Of great value is the fact that we know under whose mandate the *diakonoi* operate: that is, the *episkopoi*. So long as some people were functioning as *episkopoi*, the *diakonoi* had a role and a public identity. We say this because, from the nature of the terms, *episkopoi* could operate without *diakonoi*, but *diakonoi* could not operate without some such mandating functionary as an *episkopos*. Of equal value is the religious background of so much of the Greek usage, a context which is exactly mirrored in the particularly religious level of the language employed by Paul in this letter.

This allows us to say confidently that even though the task which warrants the use of the title in Philippi is not of the same ranking as the task warranting Paul's claim to the title, the religious character of the task can hardly be less. Paul was enormously conscious of the quality of blessing which constituted a group as a gathering of believers in Christ. So much was this the case that his constant designation of the members was 'the holy ones, the saints', and in few other places in his writings is this sense of holiness so pervasive as in this letter. Thus this lends a religious dimension to both titles *episkopoi* and *diakonoi* at the beginning of the letter just as these two titles – or at least certainly the title *diakonoi* – contribute to the religious character of the composition as a whole.

A title

Given that Paul's writing here provides us with a richly ornamented framework in which to set our understanding of Philippi's *diakonoi*, it is greatly to our loss that he did not have occasion to sketch in the details of who these functionaries were. The only information we seem able to glean is that they were assistants in some religious capacity to their *episkopoi*.

We do not know, however, if the *episkopoi* and *diakonoi* carried the titles on a permanent or on a temporary basis. We do not even know for certain if the titles were assigned to the functionaries by the Philippians, for it is not beyond imagining that Paul could have applied the titles in an honorific sense to mark a particular occasion. In the case of *episkopoi*, a word not otherwise used by him, such is perhaps not likely to be the case. In the case of *diakonoi*, on the other hand, it is conceivable that Paul would wish to honour by a suitably religious designation the individuals whom he knew to have been consistently of assistance to the *episkopoi*.

Characteristic gatherings

Of course, even on the basis of the little we do know about Philippi and the early Christian movement, we are perhaps in a position to make surmises about what circumstances could have led to the pairing of these two titles.

The communal activity most characteristic of churches – or 'gatherings' – in Pauline foundations was the meal associated with teaching and prayer. As well, the evidence is clear that the meals were held in the houses of those well enough endowed to provide space for the numbers involved. Paul's concern about the appropriate ways of conducting these meals is also well known from his reactions to certain practices in Corinth (1 Corinthians 10:11 — 11:34). His overriding practical principle for the conduct of the gathering was the maintaining of good order. Grounding this was the spiritual conviction that the gathering constituted the body of Christ and that the occasion functioned solely for the purpose of making that body stronger – the 'upbuilding' upon which he so strongly insists.

When we consider what he had to say about upbuilding, we find him advising that it would best occur by way of sound teaching shared and reflected upon. This is the practice of which he provided so vivid a picture in his advice throughout 1 Corinthians 14. His concern there is for the sensible regulation of rather spectacular forms of prayer in unintelligible 'tongues'. The whole scene suggests more than enough reason for the occasion to be under the wise guidance of a president or 'overseer'. Could this have been the role of the *episkopoi* in Philippi?

In Philippi there could well have been more than one household in the city which was made available for Christian gatherings, each with its overseer and each overseer with assistants. In Romans 16 we read fairly clear signs that several households provided gathering places for the Christians of Rome. The people named there, together with associated family members, would themselves have formed a sizeable crowd for any one household, and since Paul's list was not a census of all believers in the city many more would have swelled those numbers.

As it is, we read of one church in the house of Prisca and Aquila (16:5). Elsewhere in the list we read of a group associated with Narcissus (16:11), of 'all the saints' associated with the couple Philologus and Julia, with Nereus and his sister, and with Olympas (16:15). For good measure Paul closes this list with greetings from 'all the churches of Christ', these being presumably the churches in his place of writing. Perhaps the single church in Philippi that Paul had reason to be grateful to (Philippians 4:15) had built up in an intervening period to such an extent as to require meetings in more than one place, each requiring the guidance of its overseer and deacons.

A relational title

If such were the background of Paul's reference to these titular figures, we would need to bear in mind that the *diakonos* would be so named by reason of the relationship with the *episkopos*. This is already clear from the association of the two titles in the address of the letter. As a result, the titular value of the word is antecedent to any activity in which the *diakonos* might become involved. Unless we give this factor due weight, we could easily become side-tracked into thinking prematurely of the *diakonos* as necessarily or automatically a waiter at tables. We will see that, later, Ignatius of Antioch discards any such identification of the specific role of deacon, but of course we have no knowledge of any connection between custom in his time and place with custom among Christians in Philippi. Realistically, given what we know in general of Greek custom at meals, the waiting upon the guests would quite fittingly be in the hands of the young, if not indeed of slaves like Onesimus, who came from a household where a church met (Philemon 2). But of such details, like much else in the life of the first churches, we will never know.

Deacons in scattered churches

As we move into a later stratum of early Christian writings we gain glimpses into communities whose situations are in some ways more clearly defined than in the Pauline communities of the middle of the first century.

Fluid patterns

One feature of life in these communities at the turn of the century is the need they felt to look back upon their traditions and to measure their fidelity to what they had received. This attitude expresses itself in several instructions to maintain the purity of teaching. On the other hand we also encounter a seemingly contrary tendency, which exhibits itself in reports of visiting teachers who are sometimes called apostles or prophets. In scholarly discussion they are commonly styled wandering teachers, but scholars do not have sufficient evidence to determine where they originated or on what grounds their teaching may have been authenticated. Some reports suggest that these figures were indeed prophetic in character, drawing their inspiration from their experience of the Spirit. Hence we read of them also as charismatic teachers.

Even so, as with the prophets whose leadership Paul encouraged at gatherings of the Corinthian community, prophets may not have practised an exclusively itinerant style but may have been residents in their communities of origin and have been drawn by their prayerful experience there to make occasional pastorally inspired visits to other neighbouring communities. There is no necessity to think of them – and no evidence to lead us to think of them – as ranging far and wide across the loose network of Christian communities over the length and breadth of the eastern Mediterranean world.

As 'apostles' they may well have been encouraged by their own communities to take their particular insights to other communities. I mention such possibilities because much of the literature which an interested reader would encounter in following up Christian writings of the period – documents like the *Didache* or the *Shepherd* of Hermas – can be confusing. This is especially likely to be the case, given the confidence with which editors of these documents construct conflicting patterns of the evolution of roles of leadership within these early Christian communities.

Shadowy patterns

The generally-preferred picture that emerges from scholarship is that after a generation or two, during which the mainspring of community life lay in the spiritual energies and teachings of charismatically-endowed individuals, an alternative leadership began to develop in the interests of stability. The object would have been to establish a considered continuity with the past. This leadership would eventually emerge in the form of bishops, presbyters and deacons, although the stages at which this threefold system developed again remain unclear, and their arrangement was strongly debated among scholars through the early twentieth century.

On one theory the threefold system was a compromise between two pre-existing systems, one simply a leadership of presbyters or elders, under the inspiration of the Jewish system, and the other the paired leadership of bishops and deacons, supposedly a preference among Greeks. The latter hypothesis is further complicated because, as reflections on Paul's letter to Philippi have already illustrated, bishops or *episkopoi* can be argued to have existed in some numbers within a local community before the system of monepiscopacy – involving only one bishop for one church – emerged and moved into history as the dominant form of leadership within institutional Christianity throughout the course of the next one and a half thousand years.

These historical hypotheses are mentioned to help us keep in mind the profound obscurity surrounding the rise of forms of church order with which the Christian world is now familiar. In the dull light cast by these hypotheses we would be advised not to attempt to draw too many firm conclusions about any of the developments nor to fashion a critique of the modern diaconate against the shadowy patterns of the era.

The pull of tradition

Within the era of the New Testament itself we sense in one document relevant to us a strong concern that patterns of behaviour and thinking should be brought under the control of a central teaching authority. This is in the first letter to Timothy. Inscribed as a letter of Paul to Timothy, and indeed addressed as by Paul to Timothy, the document has left most scholars considering it to be posthumous to Paul and the product of a church around the turn of the first century that claimed its foundation in his teaching.

Although not universally agreed, this opinion does form the majority view, so that readers need to be aware that here we are using this document as expressing concepts and evidencing practice of a Christian church that had been established for a comparatively long time. We get a feeling for a church of such a later time when we read, for example, of the author's warnings in chapter 1 against false doctrine in 'legends and interminable genealogies', and against 'hypocritical liars' and 'unholy legends' in chapter 4, or view the seemingly settled arrangements for widows and the long-standing familiarity with presbyters in chapter 5.

A further indication of a more mature organization within the community, one more fittingly ascribed to the turn of the first century than to its middle years, is the set of instructions concerning *episkopos* and *diakonoi* in chapter 3. In the light of the close association of these two titles in the much earlier letter to the Philippians, it is indeed interesting to see them cropping up in tandem again here, as they will continue to do throughout diverse later literature. On this occasion, however, we notice that the *diakonoi* stand in a relationship to a single *episkopos*, not with several as in Philippi. Whether or not the Philippian arrangement had at first been a singular innovation within that church, for some reason that would seem to lie in a connection deep within the nature of Christian communities the pair of terms reappear in the church of Timothy.

Perhaps accentuating this feature of the letter is that the term for deacon, which here does at last take on the air of a title belonging to an institution, occurs at a technical level of language while elsewhere in the letter we see the author employing two *diakon-* words in the style of Paul himself – and indeed in the style of a writer familiar with the wide-ranging applications of these words. Early in the letter the author concludes a warning against deviant doctrines with a claim to the possession of the 'wholesome teaching' of the gospel (1:3–11). The author proceeds to express gratitude to Christ the Lord for having appointed him 'to this mission of proclamation' (1:12), here expressed expertly in Greek by the simple phrase 'appointed to *diakonia*'. This is in the manner of Paul himself, who identified his mission by the same term (2 Corinthians 5:18). Again echoing Paul (for example, 1 Corinthians 3:5), the author assures Timothy that he will succeed in being 'a good *diakonos* (or messenger) of Christ Jesus' if he extends the teachings and warning to the community (4:6).

An institutional deacon

Thus, in speaking in chapter 3 of the qualities to be looked for in *diakonoi* in their relationship with an *episkopos*, the author is moving out of general rhetorical use of the term and adopting the institutional language that has developed around this pairing of bishop and deacon. This is strong evidence of a major organizational development already well in place. The *episkopos* unmistakably appears as the pre-eminent of the two because of his singularity, because his 'good work' is discussed first, and because of a required qualification in teaching (3:2 'qualified to teach').

In addition, by comparison the *diakonoi* appear as having been put through some kind of apprenticeship (3:10), and their competency is then under observation to see if they might be capable of working at an apparently more responsible level in the community (3:13). Our modern translations are often not very helpful in making this clear. They often speak of the deacons as performing 'helpful service' when the Greek at both verse 10 and verse 13 is designed to speak specifically of 'carrying out one's role as a deacon', a further indication of the institutionalization of the role.

Of particular interest, in the light of the injunction against women teaching (2:11–12), is the seemingly clear case to be made for the inclusion of women among the deacons on the basis of 3:11. Here instructions very similar to those issued to the deacons now appear as applying to women before the author turns back to addressing male deacons (3:8–13). There is little to choose between the standards expected of these women and those expected of the men designated deacons. One requirement of women is that they should be 'faithful'; being *pistis* or faithful in the sense of trustworthy had been the hallmark of any *diakonos* from time immemorial. It seems simplest and best to think of the women also as deacons. One notices as well a similarity between instructions given about the *episkopos* and instructions about deacons, the only significant difference being in a requirement for a competency in teaching on the part of the *episkopos*. On this basis we might surmise that teaching was not a responsibility at this time of these deacons.

Profiling a role
To win insights into what role may have been assumed for deacons here is not easy, unless one is satisfied with the idea that the role was simply something aligned with the single *episkopos*. If in regard to Philippians 1:1 we felt that the association of the two figures could have rested on the ground of their collaboration in religious meals, we might be inclined to grasp at an indication of something similar in what the author goes on to say here. The instructions so far given concerned, firstly, public prayer (2:1) and the respective levels of participation in this by men and women (2:8–15), and, secondly, the personal qualities to be looked for in bishop and deacons, including women deacons (3:1–13). Already perhaps we have a correlation between these sets of instructions, the one about conduct during community gatherings and the other about the leader and his assistants at the gatherings.

What the author goes on to develop strengthens this impression. The author issues further instructions for the purpose of developing attitudes appropriate to 'the house of God which is the gathering [church] of the living God' (3:15). Thus the house, that is, the building where those belonging to God meet as a church, becomes God's house. Again, therefore, we have a leader and assistants in a domestic building with prayers, including prayers of thanksgiving (2:1), but very likely also with some participation in food. The author's focus, however, narrows to the teaching which would accompany the prayer gathering and to the importance of teaching in preventing aberrations (3:15–4:5); it then switches to the personal responsibility for teaching on the part of Timothy, upon whom the hands of elders had been laid (4:6–16). It might seem that the role of deacons was confined to assistance of the *episkopos* in connection with the gathering of the believers and with any common meal upon that occasion. This supposition could well be supported by the fact that participation in teaching is spoken of exclusively as a function of another group, the elders (5:17).

The Didache
The practice followed in another church of an unknown locality but of around the same period projects something like the same picture of these roles. The document is the *Didache*, a book of teachings which have been brought together from earlier sources. The teachings are thus evidence of some ageing of the practices we read of here. Their collection in the form of a book is evidence also of an interest in preserving or stabilizing teachings of an earlier period. Analysis of the *Didache* has been intense since its discovery in 1873, some conclusions about its contents contributing decisively to leading theories about the development of church order. Vigorous debate continues.

The relevant statement for us about deacons takes us back to the multiple bishops of Philippians 1:1, but the same pairing of the titles further strengthens the close association with *episkopoi*. The main interest is in the additional detail concerning religious ritual. The *episkopoi* and *diakonoi* are said to perform the religious services (15:1 'liturgy') which the author says 'prophets and teachers' had once provided. These services were eucharistic. Whereas the prophets and teachers had been occasional visitors, the author is here urging that the community select and appoint residential ministers for the regular provision of the Eucharist.

Clement of Rome

The famous intervention of Clement of Rome in a long-standing dispute about liturgical presidency in Corinth at the end of the first century powerfully strengthens the liturgical bond of deacons at that period. Some aspects of the dispute are not entirely clear, but we would seem to be witnessing recommendations from Clement on its resolution. In the course of these we find that Clement builds deep-rooted analogies between the liturgical personnel of the Jewish temple and the Christian leadership in Corinth. Among the leaders we read of *'episkopoi* and deacons' whom the ancient apostles had reputedly appointed in the first instance (42.4).

The leadership also included presbyters, however. Indeed the leadership was constituted of them, and from among their number were appointed the ones to assume presidency or *episkopē* of the eucharist. Interestingly, at this point of direct discussion of the liturgy, Clement speaks of presidency rather than of president or bishop, leading us to think that management and supervision of the church lay with the body of presbyters. Presidency or *episcopē* was something different. It was an exclusively liturgical responsibility and devolved in turn upon individual members of the presbyterate. In their role as liturgical leaders, however, presbyters were attended by deacons, whose character is once again seemingly determined by their connection with people who took on the role of *episkopoi* for the purpose of providing liturgy for the community.

The martyr Justin

Some decades later, another writer, Justin the martyr, in presenting a defence of Christian life against prejudicial assumptions of outsiders, made the liturgical function the only object of his comment on deacons. He makes no mention of *episkopoi* at this point but does report a president conducting the liturgy at which 'those we call deacons' distribute eucharistic bread and wine. This they also later take to absent members (*Apologia* 1.65.5).

Polycarp

Like Justin, Polycarp, who is reported as having died in 155 CE, makes no mention of *episkopoi* in his letter to the Philippians. The letter conveys exhortations to various sectors of the community, including women, widows, deacons, young men, young women and presbyters. The presbyters are instructed to take care of widows, orphans, and the destitute, whereas the deacons receive only exhortations to virtuous living. They are reminded, however, that they are 'deacons of God and of Christ, not of men' (5.2), a teaching reflected in the final exhortation to 'walk according to the truth of the Lord, who became *diakonos* of all'. In this possible allusion to Mark 9:35, Polycarp is providing the Lord as the absolute standard of how *diakonoi* must carry out the will of the God and Christ, whose deacons they are. The phrase is not saying that the role of deacons is to engage themselves in the service of all the people.

A bond established

While these documents have been consistent in establishing a bond between *episkop-* and deacon, a bond most clearly discernible in relation to liturgical activities, they have been obscure or ambiguous about the relationship between the pair named *'episkopoi* and deacons', on the one hand, and presbyters or 'prophets and teachers' on the other. Nor do the documents tell us anything explicit about other possible aspects of the role of deacons.

The Shepherd of Hermas

Only one document, *The Shepherd* of Hermas, turns the tables here, giving brief indications of responsibilities of deacons in the handling of moneys destined for the support of widows and orphans; on the other hand, it has nothing to say in relation to liturgy. The same is to be said of its comments on *episkopoi*, with whom, however, a relationship is clearly in evidence.

The silence about liturgy in this document is to be

explained against its underlying concern about the damage inflicted on the church by failures of morality. All levels of membership of the church are put under scrutiny in this regard, and by reason of their handling of community finances both bishops and deacons are exposed to invitations to underhand dealings. The interesting thing is that suspicions are directed at deacons, not at *episkopoi*, suggesting that the later tendency to assign business affairs to deacons was already in place in the situation known by the author.

Deacons in churches Ignatius knew

The letters of Ignatius of Antioch make good reading for deacons but difficult reading for historians. By tradition Ignatius was third bishop of Antioch of Syria, a city which, with Alexandria, was one of the three great cities of the Roman empire and headquarters of the important and rich eastern provinces. Deported to Rome for public execution, which reportedly occurred in 108 CE, Ignatius wrote letters of encouragement and farewell to several churches during his final journey. The letters have constituted a major source of information on the order observed in ancient churches. Although historians and theologians do not all share the same level of enthusiasm for the reliability of the information, from a linguistic point of view the Greek language of the letters does provide a window on to one early Christian estimation of the role and status of the deacon in the ancient Middle East. It is for this we use the letters.

Focus on language

One reason many theologians express reservations about the value of the letters of Ignatius for the study of church order today is that the churches we encounter in these documents are just too well ordered. Here, supposedly in the earliest years of the second century, we have a settled hierarchy in place across six cities of Asia Minor. The hierarchy consisted of one bishop, a number of presbyters, and a number of deacons. All these churches were clear embodiments of the monepiscopacy which characterized the great Constantinian and medieval churches. In Ignatius the pattern is obvious and uniform, unlike the vague outlines of leadership and indications of variation provided in documents already referred to which are possibly contemporary or later and whose place of origin could not have been far removed from Asia Minor.

Mindful of limitation, we are able, nonetheless, to perceive in the language of the letters the values which an ancient author attached to words about deacons. Thus our purpose in using these letters is not – as was often the case throughout most of the last century – to look for models of a diaconate for today but to take from the ancient language itself some indications of how some people once conceived of deacons. Perceptions here can point to principles by which the ancient diaconate functioned.

Shared slavery

The bishop Ignatius champions deacons every time he mentions them, and in a notable gesture expresses a sense of the personal bond between himself as bishop and the deacons of the various churches. The hints of an inherent bond between bishop and deacon, which other early documents provide, find full and considered expression in Ignatius. (The bond is so strongly expressed, in fact, that scholars have occasionally attempted to argue that Ignatius was a deacon himself instead of the bishop he calls himself in *Romans* 2.2.) With a strong sense of himself as a slave (*doulos*) of God, he is fond of reminding the deacons whom he addresses that they are his co-slaves (*syndouloi*). With this, we are at once raised to the level at which the whole of Ignatius' discourse proceeds. This is a level where the church is infused with the holiness and blessing of God, and all language expresses aspects of the blessed state in which its members live or aspects of the appropriate behaviour such blessing invites.

The most obvious external feature of the order Ignatius alludes to is that it consists of three levels of bishop, presbyters and deacons. The titles are always mentioned in that order. To these the people are instructed to submit themselves for governance and teaching. Sometimes the submission is expressed as due to the bishop and presbyters, and sometimes, even in the same letter, to all three. Thus the people appear as little more than subjects under a threefold governing structure.

In regard to the relationships of the deacons within the threefold order, Ignatius instances the deacon Zotion standing in relation to the bishop as to 'the grace of God' and to the presbyters as to 'the law of God'. These expressions are from the opening of the letter to the Magnesians (2). In this letter the author later reflects on the religious orientation of each of the three levels. The bishop presides over the local church in the place of God, and the presbyters in the place of the council of the apostles, while the deacons – 'my dearest deacons' – are entrusted with 'the *diakonia* of Jesus Christ' (*Magnesians* 6.1).

This is an interesting expression, and illustrates the value of reading these documents for the light that the language throws upon an ancient perception of the diaconate. As an expression here, 'the *diakonia* of Jesus Christ' is designating the role assigned to the Son of Man in Mark's phrase, 'to *serve* (*diakon-*) and give his life as a ransom' (Mark 10:45). That is to say, Mark presented the Son of Man *as carrying out a commission from God*. Expressed as a noun, this commission is called a *diakonia*. Used to designate the role of the deacon, whose very title is also a *diakon-* word, *diakonia* similarly designates the deacon's *commission from God*. Because, however, as Ignatius has already purposely stated, the bishop stands 'in the place of God', the deacon's *diakonia* becomes a *commission to carry out the will of the bishop*.

A theological portrait

In the presence of such a seemingly rigid structure, so repugnant to modern aspirations for a church of the People of God, perhaps we need to bear in mind that the writer has framed a theological rather than a managerial structure. In fact, as we see from the theological model of the presbyterate presented in the preceding phrase, the bishop acts only within the ambit of 'the council of the apostles'. The bishop is thus not quite the autocrat one might hesitate to accept in a church today. What the theological framework does bring to the fore, however, is the meaning which ancients understood as being inherent in the title of the deacon. This is that the deacon's orientation is towards the needs of the church as discerned by the wisest counsel it possesses in its appointed ministers. Even there we need to bear in mind that congregations of Christians in Hellenistic cities of first century Asia Minor were not made up of politically-sensitive citizens of our modern democracies.

The writer projects the same pattern of interrelationships in the letter to the Trallians (3.1). Respect is owing to the bishop as representing to the church the divine Father, to the presbyters as 'the council of God and band of apostles', and to the deacons 'as Jesus Christ' himself. Ignatius' insistence on the correlation between deacon and Jesus Christ arises from his perception of Jesus doing only what his Father willed. He draws expressly on this concept in addressing an exhortation to the whole church of Smyrna 'to follow the bishop in the way that Jesus Christ obeys the Father' (8.1). In the same exhortation all are to respect the deacons 'as the command of God', which is another way of saying that in what deacons do they are carrying out the will of God as discerned and formulated by the council of presbyters and bishop.

The church's executives

The same perception underlies what is perhaps Ignatius' most familiar statement about deacons. On several occasions we have alluded to the fact that a Greek-speaking audience was familiar with the public roles of *diakonoi* as waiters. We have also referred to the association which other early Christian documents seem to maintain between deacons and eucharistic liturgies. In writing to the Trallians, Ignatius advises that, by force of this association, he does not want the Christian deacons confused with the *diakonoi* of the public festivals or indeed with the *diakonoi* who might operate at the Christian religious banquets in the homes of the wealthy. Firstly, by stating that the church's deacons are 'deacons of the mysteries of Christ', he is placing them within the church's living awareness of the death and resurrection; these are 'the mysteries' which he identifies in the letter to the Magnesians (9.1) and which are commemorated in the eucharistic liturgy.

To make it clear that the deacon's identity arises from the community born of these mysteries and not merely from ritual connected with the celebration of the mysteries in bread and wine, Ignatius goes on to state, secondly, that deacons 'are not waiters (*diakonoi*) providing food and drink, but are executives (*hypēretai*) of the church of God' (*Trallians* 2.3). The Greek-speaking audience was familiar with the word *hypēretai;* this was their term for the clerks of court and the minor officials who make government effective in any civil administration. By making this allusion here Ignatius is indicating once again that the Christian deacon's title has not originated in a correlation to the practical needs of people but is a religious title appropriate to a functionary who operates within a body with a high sense of its holiness and who carries out the resolutions of its holy council.

In addressing the church's use of the eucharistic liturgy in the letter to the Philadelphians, Ignatius conveys a strong sense of where the deacon stands in relation to the community. He writes (4.1): 'Take care to use only one eucharist, for the flesh of Jesus Christ is one, the cup for union with his blood is one, and the altar is one, just as there is one bishop in union with the presbyters and the deacons, who are my co-slaves.' The liturgy, in other words, is the expression of the oneness of the church, at whose centre deacons stand to assist those whose responsibility it is to make the ritual oneness real.

Deacons entering history

History, from the viewpoint of deacons, gets under way only in the late fourth century, and then puts deacons in an unflattering light. Around 375 CE an unknown author launched a tract – *On the arrogance of deacons* – against the high station which Rome's seven deacons had assumed in the clerical world of Rome at the expense of the city's much more numerous presbyters. The deacons had been seven in number since at least the decision of Pope Fabian in the middle of the third century to divide the city for administrative purposes into seven regions and to place a deacon over each.

The number seven

The number seven owes its origin, of course, to the belief that Luke's story in the sixth chapter of the Acts of the Apostles was about the ordination of seven deacons. Irenaeus of Lyons is the first known to have promulgated this view towards the end of the second century, but soon enough it was the universal belief, as evidenced by canon 15 of the synod of Neocaesarea around 315 CE In fact this canon merely promulgated a pre-existing regulation: 'Deacons must be only seven in number, according to the law. This may be proved from the Acts of the Apostles.'

With such a small number of deacons in a city as large as Rome, the administrative responsibilities which they had to carry were considerable. One consequence of this was that less substantial duties began to be allocated to new and lesser members of an expanding clerical caste. Thus subdeacons and porters and acolytes assumed roles in the organization of the assembly for liturgy. The people most immediately affected by the changing roles among personnel responsible for liturgy were of course the presbyters, whose responsibility it was to preside at the liturgies. For better or for worse some of the presbyters took umbrage at what they interpreted as the arrogance of the deacons in abdicating liturgical responsibilities for which they had been ordained.

Such may have been one reason for the sense of grievance which had developed among presbyters. Closer to the nub, however, was the fact that as a matter of course deacons had been succeeding to the bishopric of Rome. Indeed for a deacon to be advanced to ordination as a presbyter came to be recognized as a sign that he was not in line of succession. This arrangement for the succession is actually further evidence of the bond between bishops and deacons, illustrating that deacons were adjudged to have gathered the appropriate experience through close collaboration with the bishop to earn a recommendation for selection. But the arrangement did nothing to strengthen bonds between deacons and presbyters. The conflict which flared on this ground would lead in the next centuries to the heightening of the profile and prestige of the presbyters and to the demise of the diaconate.

Human factors

This story is the human side of unfortunate changes in the pastoral functions of the church. Once the number of deacons was limited to seven, their pastoral value in the church diminished in adverse proportion to the growth of congregations. As congregations increased in number, deacons became less visible at the same time as presbyters were more and more in evidence in liturgical and pastoral activities. In the face of large sociological changes the church did nothing to support or expand the pastoral relevance of the deacons. One is inclined to judge that the period of fruitful contribution of deacons to the real purposes of the church was already past. However, the kind of information we have about the life and role of deacons in the second and third centuries unfortunately does not allow us to arrive at a reliable evaluation of the diaconate in the church of those periods.

Among factors we need to bear in mind, nonetheless, is the profile of Christian congregations during that period. In 303 Diocletian issued the first of numerous letters across the empire which were aimed at the extermination of the Christian sect. The church historian Eusebius points out that just prior to this alarming development the numbers in the congregations were increasing rapidly and that grand buildings – 'dominical basilicas' – had to be built to accommodate them. These were all to be razed. In Nicomedia, the imperial centre in the East, Diocletian stood in the company of his co-ruler watching mobs attack the new Christian building. The two emperors discussed setting fire to the basilica but fear for the safety of neighbouring property deterred them. So they sent in the Praetorian Guard to effect a total demolition.

Imperial officers also searched out volumes of scriptures in the homes of presbyters and lectors. Finds were recorded, 'some pastors of the churches hiding shamefully here and there,' recorded Eusebius, while others were led away to take the test of pagan sacrifice under pain of instant death or brutal tortures. In one interrogation we read:

> The proconsul said, 'In your house the congregation had been gathered contrary to the order of the emperors?'
>
> Since Emeritus was filled with the Holy Spirit, he said, 'In my house we conducted the Lord's Supper.'
>
> The proconsul asked, 'Why did you permit them to enter?'
>
> Emeritus answered, 'Because they are my brothers, and I cannot prohibit them.'
>
> 'But you should have stopped them.'
>
> 'Certainly not,' said Emeritus, 'for it is not possible for us to exist without the Lord's Supper.'

On Diocletian's premature retirement, the fortunes of Christians rapidly changed. Decree followed decree offering them compensation for property lost, and the building of great edifices once more got under way. Total freedom was guaranteed and, by the end of the fourth century, the Christian religion became the religion of the state. That dubious achievement coincided with the public attack in Rome on the integrity of the seven deacons.

A crowded room
Thus, at the time of this internal tension, the experience of Christians as a public religion was not extensive. The *Didascalia Apostolorum*, a writing on church order about 280, immediately prior to the sudden expansion of the church before the onslaught of Diocletian, projects an unsophisticated air in the scene it presents of a gathering. Even in the following abridged extract from an English translation (Connolly, 1929) of a Syriac original, we are clearly in the presence of a group of people who, for all the high sense of reverence they seek to cultivate, are worshipping in simple and unpretentious surroundings. When the people assemble, there is standing room only, and even then much shuffling to make room for others.

> You bishops, gather the faithful with much patience, and with doctrine and exhortation, as ministers of the kingdom everlasting. Hold your assemblies with all decent order, and appoint the places for the brethren with care and gravity.
>
> And for the presbyters let there be assigned a place in the eastern part of the house; and let the bishop's throne be set in their midst, and let the presbyters sit with him.
>
> But of the deacons let one stand always by the oblations of the Eucharist; and let another stand without by the door and observe them that come in; and afterwards, when you offer, let them minister together in the church.
>
> And if any one be found sitting out of his place, let

the deacon who is within reprove him and make him to rise up and sit in a place that is meet for him. And let the deacon also see that no one whispers, or falls asleep, or laughs, or makes signs.

For so it should be, that with decency and decorum they watch in the church, with ears attentive to the word of the Lord. But if, while young men or women sit, an older man or woman should rise and give up their place, do thou, O deacon, scan those who sit, and see which man or woman of them is younger than the rest, and make them stand up, and cause him to sit who had risen and given up his place; and him whom thou hast caused to stand up, lead away and make him to stand behind his neighbours: that others also may be trained and learn to give place to those more honourable than themselves.

But if a poor man or woman should come, especially if they are stricken in years, and there be no place for such, do thou, O bishop, with all thy heart provide a place for them, even if thou have to sit upon the ground; that thou be not as one who respects the persons of men, but that thy ministry may be acceptable with God.

Forty-seven pairs of shoes

In surviving records of the second and third centuries evidences of the history of these people – as opposed to the writings of a number of their philosophers and apologists – are comparatively sparse. Legendary accounts of early Christian heroes speak occasionally of 'a gathering in the house of Onesiphorus' or 'in the house of the deacon Xenophon'. The first written record of a church building is said to be from the year 200 in the writings of Clement of Alexandria. Perhaps a typical congregation in a provincial city would consist of the 80 women and 20 or so men whose presence we detect in the following records of the Roman mayor of Cirta (in the region of today's Tunisia) on 19 May 303:

When they arrived at the house in which the Christians would assemble, Felix, the mayor, said to Paul, the bishop, 'Bring out the writings of the law and anything else you have here, as was ordered, so that you may obey the law'.

Paul, the bishop, said, 'The readers have the scriptures, but we will give you what we have here.'

Felix, the mayor, said, 'Point out the readers or send for them.'

Paul, the bishop, said, 'You all know them.'

Felix, the mayor, said, 'We do not know them.'

Paul, the bishop, said, 'The public office, that is the clerks Edusius and Junius, knows them.'

Felix, the mayor, said, 'Holding over the matter of the readers, whom the office will point out, hand over whatever you have.'

In the presence of the bishop Paul, seated, with Montanus and Victor Deusatelius and Memorius, the presbyters, and standing by Martis and Helios, the deacons, with Marculius, Catullinus, Silvanus, and Carosus, the subdeacons, and with Januarius, Meraclus, Fructuosus, Migginis, Saturninus, Victor, and the rest … (they brought out) before the scribe Victor of Aufidus, who wrote in brief as follows: 2 gold cups, 6 silver cups, 6 silver pitchers, a small silver kettle, 7 silver lamps, 2 wax candles, 7 small bronze lamps with their wicks, 11 bronze lamps with chains, 82 women's tunics, 38 [veils], 16 men's tunics, 13 pairs of men's shoes, 47 pairs of women's shoes, and 19 crude [sandals].

Pitiful as these people are in their vulnerability before the imperial decrees, and patent, as the full further record shows, their nobility – even in these terrifying circumstances the bishop is seated with his elders, the deacons standing in attendance – such were the congregations of the times. They met for Eucharist and for the Scriptures. In this instance the findings added up to 33 volumes – these would have been sections of the Bible – located in eight different households.

A real church

Since 1934 we have had the extraordinary benefit of being able to examine the arrangements in one such household which had actually been adapted to accommodate its congregation. This was in Dura-Europos, a prominent city of central Syria in the years before its destruction by Persian forces. Constructed as a residence in 232, it was then renovated in 241 to function exclusively as a *domus ecclesiae* or 'house of a congregation' until the end of the city in 256.

The sites of a few other *domus ecclesiae* are known but the buildings themselves have virtually disappeared under the development of permanent churches on their base. War was to ensure that this would never be the case for the house church in Dura-Europos. Here we have a house standing on a domestic block, slightly larger than most in the city, some 17.5 x 20 metres in size. A discreet entry from the street opened upon a central courtyard. Rooms faced on to the court from four sides. On one side two rooms of the residence had been transformed into one small hall measuring nearly 13 metres in length and over 5 metres in width, sufficient to accommodate some 120 adults.

On the opposite side of the courtyard had been a small room which the Christians transformed into a baptistery. They adorned its plastered surfaces with frescoes depicting scenes from the gospels. Here was the home of believers, supported and nurtured by scriptures which those among them who could read preserved. They were instructed by their teachers, and organized for their liturgies by those who presided over them: not a large group of people, and not one of them unknown to another.

Lawrence

The sociology of the churches in Rome would have been more complex. The numbers would have made it so. But within two years of the violent end of the congregation of Dura-Europos, scenes unfolded in Rome which have been permanently etched in the memory of the Western church. These are from the final days in the life of the deacon Lawrence. He was deacon to Pope Xystus, who became bishop of Rome in 257 and had ordained Lawrence as the first of the seven serving in the city. Lawrence was closest to Xystus, and was entrusted with the treasury. When Xystus was apprehended in 258 and was being led to his execution, Lawrence accompanied him but was not himself arrested. He is said to have complained to the bishop of being separated from him in death: 'Whither are you going, holy priest, without your deacon? You never went to offer sacrifice without me, your minister.'

The story unfolds further, as our memory reminds us. A short time later, the prefect of the city charged Lawrence to produce the wealth of which he was the custodian. When the prefect was confronted with a crowd of the destitute of Rome heralded by the deacon as the treasure of the church, Lawrence was himself apprehended and cruelly burnt to death over a slow fire. This was four days after the execution of Xystus.

We have never forgotten who the treasure of the church is. But in thinking of the deacon Lawrence in modern times we have usually overlooked what he understood his distinguishing mark to be. This was his association with the bishop and his function by the bishop's side as the congregation came together to celebrate its identity as a people full of blessing and memory of the Lord.

A church order

The oldest known church order is possibly *The Apostolic Tradition*. It is commonly ascribed to the priest Hippolytus, who would have composed it some thirty years before the death of Lawrence. Hippolytus was in no position to impose regulations, but he was involved in a controversy at a high level about the proper arrangements for the church in Rome. Accordingly, he was not in a position to invent novelties either. He sought in the first place to put before his opponents the ideal which the church's ministry was meant to serve. His work thus contains the invaluable reflection of what a concerned and informed Christian envisaged for its ministers.

In regard to deacons Hippolytus states succinctly that in ordination only the bishop lays hands on him 'because the deacon is not ordained to priesthood but to the service of the bishop, so that he will do what the bishop commands him'. Of great value for an understanding of this statement about the service of the deacon to the bishop is the Greek word for *service* which the editor of the Latin document supplied. The word is *hypēresia*. This word is part of the public service terminology that we encountered earlier in Ignatius of Antioch. As in Ignatius, it indicates here that the ancients thought of the deacon in effect as an executive officer of the bishop.

About this aspect of Hippolytus' statement, there is nothing religious. In the minds of the ancients, the official title of the deacon, *diakonos,* was itself a constant public statement of the religious character of this functionary. What Hippolytus' statement does is to remind us that the deacon was an agent of the one presiding over the church's liturgical and spiritual life. This is why in the prayer of ordination, the bishop prays to God as 'father of our Lord Jesus Christ whom you sent to do your will'. Jesus' conformity to the will of God forms the model of what the deacon is ordained to be.

4

Making connections

The diaconate is undergoing far-reaching re-evaluations in churches today. The re-evaluations have been occurring at the same time as churches have been moving rapidly to incorporate the diaconate within their official ministry. Many readers would feel that such a situation presents the churches with the unusual phenomenon of official decisions being taken and canonical arrangements being made before the relevant theology is in place. Some will be inclined to think that such a situation is unhealthy. In chapter 1 we have glanced at the areas in which the conflict is playing itself out. There we noted also how contemporary theologians and study groups are increasingly weighing the implications for the theology of diaconate of the linguistic study *Diakonia: Re-interpreting the Ancient Sources*.

In the light of the findings of that book and of writings associated with it we have now reviewed the main passages of the New Testament which are usually considered to be of direct relevance to the current review of the diaconate. We have also looked at the history of early churches to observe something of the circumstances attending the development of the diaconate in that obscure era. The overall purpose is to identify within these sources those elements which we would expect churches to want to deploy in their contemporary re-evaluation of the diaconate.

The elements we might discern in the ancient sources are not, of course, the only elements that need to be considered. Today's theology works from today's needs as well, and, in particular, from perceptions arising from the experience of deacons. As we have emphasized, however, and as will be plain from the following considerations, the New Testament does have something to say about the diaconate. Across the last 150 years much has been made of one reading of these sources, and now is the time for another. Whatever we make of it, no one should dispute that the church will always begin its reflection there. Our hope is that here we can point to relevant elements arising from the New Testament and the early tradition which might contribute to resolving theological uncertainties and tensions of today. Currently these are hampering the development of a theology of diaconate with which churches and deacons can feel at ease.

A changing model

Before engaging that task, we need to be reminded of what we are not attempting to do. We are not looking for models from the past to which today's diaconate is expected to conform. We will, however, be trying to isolate factors which contributed to the understanding of the diaconate in its earliest period. What we conclude from this brief review is that we should attempt to correct a bias which developed in the theology of diaconate precisely as a result of an earlier attempt to construct a theology of the diaconate on an ancient model. The nineteenth-century diaconate of the Lutheran and Reformed tradition sought to represent in their various diaconal institutions what they considered the essence of the ancient diaconate to have been. Indeed they envisaged this as expressing the essence of what Jesus undertook to model for his disciples across the generations.

From this initial perception developed a diaconate that

was non-clerical, non-ordained, largely female, and based in the culture of the Motherhouses. Here women lived in community – as did the lesser number of men – more or less after the manner of Roman Catholic sisters. This movement, however, was not integrated into the theology of the church or into the life of the congregation. Throughout the course of this large social experiment the movement clung to the ancient titles of deacon and deaconess both as a reminder to deacons themselves of the call to which they were responding, and as a witness to the church and to those on the margins of the church.

During the second half of the twentieth century, however, in a search for re-integration into the church, the institutional forms of this diaconate progressively made more and more room for symbols of the diaconate which had survived across the centuries within different traditions. To different degrees in various regions this push included moving out of Motherhouses, closer involvement in parish life and liturgy, an entry into clerical life – this often marked by way of a distinctive form of clerical dress – and increasing pressure for official recognition as part of the ordained ministry. In places the push was for recognition within a threefold order of ministry of bishop, priest and deacon. Deacons were claiming allegiance to the tradition of which Lawrence of Rome had been the perennial symbol.

A persistent theology

Throughout what has now become an increasingly rapid development along these lines the conviction has remained almost universal that the character of diaconate remains what it was in the institutions, namely, a selfless loving service. This has remained strong at the same time as the diaconal movement has also developed increasingly sophisticated methods of delivering its services in medical care, counselling, youth and aged support, and in many other specialized areas of social welfare.

Against this trend, chapter 2 of this book, *The Diakonia of*

Jesus and the Early Church, seeks to show that it is no longer possible to continue claiming social work as an expression of what the early church meant by the term *diakonia.* Many theologians and practitioners of the modern *diakonia* disregard this disclaimer. In doing so, however, they are inviting deacons and the rest of the church to read certain passages in the New Testament in ways which the biblical authors certainly did not have in mind. Some of these passages are important to the church today for an understanding of itself and of its operations at this juncture of its history. As a result, at times and in certain situations the application of particular biblical passages to aspects of deacons' lives and work becomes a matter of trivializing biblical teachings which should be working their actual and sometimes profound theological value within the church.

We take the critical passage of Mark 10:45 by way of illustration. To present Mark's statement 'the Son of Man … came to serve' as an expression of the deacon's call to provide loving service to those in need is to impoverish Mark's theology of Jesus. Mark is here presenting Jesus, not as serving people, but as serving God. Mark's intention was to teach the church of his day that it too must be ready to die for its confession of 'the gospel of Jesus Christ, Son of God' (Mark 1:1). Many a homily will continue to misapply this passage from the gospels for the convenience of some immediate pastoral situation, but to misread it in the theology of the institutions of the church would seem to be inflicting a damage on the church itself.

Scriptures for the church
With a problem of this kind in mind, chapter 2 above was reminding us that if churches are looking for a more secure theological footing on which to build the diaconate today a basic requirement is to be particularly discerning in reading passages that use *diakon-* words. This Greek stem underlies the word used in all languages for the title of the church's deacon. But this fact does not necessarily

mean that any Greek statement using *diakon-* has immediate relevance to the theology or practice of the diaconate
today.

Following are certain well-known passages of the New
Testament which contain *diakon-* words but which do not
apply directly to the diaconate. The notes appended to
each section repeat what has already been explained in
chapter 2. This is for the purpose of emphasizing the direct
relevance of these passages to the church itself.

Mark 10:45	'the Son of man also came … to serve and give his life as a ransom for many.'
Luke 22:27	'I am among you as one who serves.'
Matthew 25:44	'When did we see you hungry … and not minister to you?'

- These passages contain teaching that is directed to
  the church as a whole. Note that, although Luke sets
  up the Last Supper as a scene between Jesus and the
  apostles (22:14 and 28–30), the scene is first and foremost for the instruction of the whole community as to
  the nature of the church and the relationship of Jesus
  to it. The *diakon-* words in these passages do not
  derive from a new and distinctive Christian vernacu-
  lar, nor do they refer in any way to acts of loving
  service.

- In drawing on the broader theological and ethical
  teaching in these passages as a support in their
  calling, deacons will enrich their understanding of

the church and of themselves as disciples within it, but they will not be drawing on anything which can be considered specifically diaconal.

Acts 6:1–6	'These [seven men] they set before the apostles, and they prayed and laid their hands upon them.'

- This passage about the seven who were selected 'to minister at tables' teaches the church that it must always put arrangements in place to extend the ministry of the word to those who look for it but are not hearing it. In this case those people were the Hellenistic widows.

- The church learns from this passage the responsibility of the congregation to assess what the ministerial needs are, how to meet them, and whom to select as appropriate ministers.

- The church also learns that it must adapt its ministry to the changing times.

- The church needs to maintain order in its ministry to help ensure its integrity across changing generations.

- The passage thus declares the place of ordained or commissioned ministers in the church – including deacons – but does not speak specifically of deacons or of diaconal tasks.

Romans 15:25	'I am going to Jerusalem on a mission from the saints.'
Romans 16:1	'I commend to you our sister Phoebe, a delegate of the church at Cenchreae...'
1 Corinthians 15:16	'the household of Stephanas has committed itself to a mission for the saints'

- These passages – and those linked with Romans 15:25 on pp. 66–77 above – illustrate the understanding which various congregations of Christians held concerning their corporate identity, their corporate relationship with other congregations, and corporate responsibilities arising from this understanding.

- The *diakon-* words occur in conventional Greek patterns to indicate that a sacred delegation is involved, sometimes with and sometimes without the delivery of goods.

- Deacons thus learn that a distinguishing mark of the ancient churches was to maintain ecclesial connections. Deacons may consider it important to build a sense of corporate responsibility into their ministry, but such a development would be essentially ecclesial in character and not specifically diaconal.

Scriptures and Tradition for deacons

In contrast to the passages reviewed in chapter 2, the passages considered in chapter 3 *The Diakonia of Early Deacons* provide deacons with teaching or perceptions which relate directly to their identity in the church. The passages include the following from both the New Testament and other early Christian documents. Again appended notes emphasize the particular reference of these passages, which, in these cases, is to the diaconate itself.

Philippians 1:1   'to the overseers and their attendants'

- While we do not think that these 'attendants' are deacons, the Greek word is *diakonoi,* and provides deacons with an opportunity to reflect on some specific characteristics of their title.

- By force of the Greek language, the title implies that the deacon stands in a relationship to a person or institution that has commissioned the deacon to a status and a task.

- Here the relationship is to 'overseers'. Whether the individuals were established in this relationship by the overseers themselves or by 'the saints', the situation also establishes the attendants in a relationship to 'the saints' or community.

- The status implied by the title brings the deacon within the sphere and authority of the commissioning authority; as a result the deacon's task carries the authority it requires.

- Deacons are part of a congregation, are known to a congregation, and stand in permanent relationship to it. Deacons are thus essentially ecclesial persons.

- The title is also a religious term, reminding deacons that they share in the holiness in which all members of the congregation of 'the saints' participate.

- Tasks of the deacon will be an extension of the reality and benefits of this holiness.

---

1 Timothy 3:1–13   'a bishop must be above reproach
... Deacons likewise ...'

- In addition to perceptions taken from Philippians 1:1, deacons learn here of a particular conviction in some early congregations, namely, that a single bishop might benefit from a body of deacons. The same might be a useful understanding within other (non-episcopal) forms of church leadership.

- The deacons could be women or men, even at the end of the first century when, as this letter also teaches, women were to be silent in the assemblies (2:8–12). (This restriction was a narrowing of practice earlier in the century in the communities established by Paul.)

- The deacon can also discern from the situation behind this passage that at times the church undergoes major change. Accordingly, deacons are to be alive to the possibilities for change. From their advantageous position within the congregation deacons ought to be available for evaluations which precede, accompany and follow change.

- Again, from their position between other leaders and other members of the congregation, they are to collaborate in multiple spheres of the process of change.

- In line with the sacred title borne by deacons, their role of assistant to a bishop or other form of church leader will find its most critical expression when the congregation gathers itself in a meeting with the Lord.

- Other documentation (Clement; Justin Martyr) supports liturgy as a prime location of the ministry of the deacon.

Ignatius, *Magnesians 6.1*   'deacons entrusted with the ministry/*diakonia* of Jesus Christ'

- Deacons are to reflect on this ancient perception that just as Jesus spent his life in total commitment (*diakonia*) to the Messianic role he had received from his Father, so the deacons live lives of total commitment (*diakonia*) to their diaconal role in and at the behest of the congregation and of the church leadership.

- Deacons are not to misread Ignatius' insistence on order as prescriptive or as a merely hierarchical arrangement. It is first and foremost a way of presenting the congregation as a holy gathering in which presbyters, that is, select members of the congregation, are in dialogue with the people, with one another, and with the bishop within the ambit of the tradition in which they stand. Deacons have a role in maintaining the community within this arrangement.

Ignatius, *Trallians 2.3*   'deacons are not waiters (*diakonoi*) providing food and drink, but are executives (*hypē retai*) of the church of God'

- Deacons are not named after any liturgical role like distributing bread and wine. They are named as – and find their identity in being – executives of the corporate leadership.

Ignatius, *Philadelphians* 4.1	'Take care to use only one euch- arist ... there is one bishop in union with the presbyters and the deacon'

- Deacons take part in the liturgy in their role of collab- orating with those whose responsibility it is to main- tain the unity of the congregation.

Synod of Neocaes- area, canon 15	'Deacons must be only seven in number... '

- This number of deacons was reached from a consid- eration of the story in Acts 6:1–6. Deacons of today are to be aware of their rights within the church and are to do all in their power to ensure that order in the church is never maintained in blind compliance with the past but is always pastorally relevant.

Defining characteristics

If we look for defining characteristics of the ancient deacon in these leading indicators from the documenta- tion, two dominant features would seem to emerge. Neither of these would seem to be prominent among char- acteristics of the modern deacon, but both would seem to offer values that could enhance the self-understanding of today's deacons.

One characteristic is that the deacon was essentially a relational figure, and we will reflect on that in terms of the deacon's connection with the church. The other character- istic arises from the fact that the deacon functioned within a community that considered itself to be living within an arena of special divine blessing. The characteristic arising from this connection we can call holiness. We need to explore a little further what these connections are saying about the ancient diaconate.

The church connection

As our bible translations across all languages have traditionally emphasized, one functionary within early churches was designated by the stable title of deacon. Because early Greek Christians chose the term *diakonos* for this title, we are immediately in a position to draw out some basic implications on the grounds of known features of Greek usage in regard to this word.

In the first place the orientation of the functionary called deacon is towards the church. At once this forms a contrast with the dominant orientation in the modern understanding of the title *diakonos*. Our contemporary orientation is towards needy situations, a position inviting the perception that the deacon is appointed as some kind of scout to discover situations of need and to take appropriate action. A model of diaconate that develops along this orientation would see the church as equipping itself with a squad of experts in social welfare and leaving them to get on with the job. They might attempt to get on with the job in groups or as lone rangers on the perimeters of church and society.

The ancient orientation, on the other hand, implies a different understanding of the deacon. Precisely because the deacon was a *diakonos,* somewhere within the church there had to be a point – a point generally identified as *episkopos* – from which a commission has issued that endows the deacon with a particular status and a set of functions. The status of *diakonos* is more significant for an understanding of the nature of the deacon than the functions, which, in any case, the sources do not spell out sufficiently clearly for us to begin from there. So we look briefly at what we can learn about the deacon's status.

Community connection

Because of the implied commission, the status remains so long as the commission is in place, and because *diakonos* quickly established itself as a title, we are to understand that the commission was a permanent one. Thus the deacon was in a permanent relationship to the commissioning agent. Although the literary and historical indications are that this relationship was in the first place to an *episkopos*, we would misrepresent the nature of the ancient congregation if we were to think of the deacon as being simply at the beck and call of a bishop. We can be quite confident about this because the overriding idea of the ancient church or congregation at the time when the *diakonos* emerged from it was that the congregation was one body; identity was corporate. The deacon or deacons were thus part of a dynamic community, a small, open community in which both personalities and communal values were known to all.

In one very early period the author of the letter to the Ephesians – a writer who, as indicated earlier, is most unlikely to have been Paul although the ideas are profoundly affected by Paul's own – gave expression to the ideal of such a community (Ephesians 4:7–16). As a result of the ministry of teaching (4:11–12), the community grows towards 'the stature of the fullness of Christ', with each single part contributing to 'the development of the body for its upbuilding in love' (4:16). The leaders of the small ancient communities in which the ministerial titles of bishop, presbyter and deacon originated were thus not leaders in a political sense, operating on principles of authority and being accountable to no one. They were fellow members of a communal undertaking to represent Christ to one another and to witness to Christ in their society. The multiple lines of communication were meant to ensure this.

Ignatius of Antioch represented this thinking accurately in the much-quoted statement that is not so frequently understood. 'Deacons are not providers (*diakonoi*) of bread and drink but are agents (*hypēretai*) of the congregation.' This dynamic orientation to the congregation of which they were part means that deacons share in the special characteristic that marked the congregation off from their society. We are constantly reminded of the characteristic in the different ways writers of the New Testament conceived of the church. The very idea of church was of those called together in the Spirit under the blessings of the Lord. For this reason Paul constantly spoke of members of the church as 'saints' or 'holy ones'. Out of their awareness of their holy status, they chose the religious term *diakonos* as a title for their agents. Not surprisingly such sacred agents are most frequently to be observed in connection with their holy rituals in commemoration of the Lord in Eucharist.

In this connection deacons were most clearly agents of the church. On the strength of this connection their further roles in the community are to be understood. The ritual of the Lord's Supper was the nourishing, fortifying and bonding action of the community, and the functionary most intimately involved in extending the benefits of the table to members of the assembly were those who were commissioned to take the benefits further, beyond the place of the assembly to absent members. This was essentially a process of extending the sphere of blessing and holiness of the assembly to those temporarily outside it, and was essentially an ecclesial action, carrying with it the authority, blessing and love of the assembly.

In his account of the Last Supper, Luke created a permanent reminder to his community of this process. The reminder consisted in nothing less than the image of the Lord himself permanently present in the middle of the remembering community 'as one who serves' at table (Luke 22:27). In a gospel narrative adorned with banquets, the Lord's Last Supper carries the essential motif of them all. Commemoration is not just of the past. Luke's commemoration is of the continuing presence of a Lord who continually summons members of the community to be present to the community in the same way that he is. They are called to extend the benefits of the commemoration as far as they will reach: the memory, the nourishment, the communion, the encouragement, the joy. From within such a commemoration the deacons are sent to be a presence like 'the one who serves' among those outside.

Educating the church

Increasingly today efforts are directed at clarifying the connection between liturgy and diaconate. On the other hand in some quarters we also observe increasingly determined efforts to resist closer ties between deacons and liturgy. It would seem that the resistance stems from a desire not to divert the diaconate from service, to which it is already deeply committed, into a clerical rank dedicated to ritual. If, however, the community itself could hear through the liturgy its own call from the Lord who serves, and who is at the centre of the ritual, the community's deacons would share a working base with members of the community. The benefit for the congregation would be the experience of a new dimension of liturgy and a fuller experience of responding to the gospel. For the deacons it would mean integration into a community and the end of the lone ranger syndrome.

It is not enough for deacons to have been once commissioned or ordained and then left to their task. This might lend deacons an ecclesiastical status, but that is not to endow them with an ecclesial identity. If the deacon is an ecclesial person, the members of the *ekklesia* or congregation need to be constantly reminded of who it is they have as their representatives beyond the liturgy. As in any true gathering, the deacons must be known among those who are gathered, and those who are gathered must understand their close bonds with those whom they send. This is a matter for prayer, reflection and collaboration, as well as of ritual.

The issue would seem to be all the more important in the light of one strong tradition within so much of the modern diaconate. This tradition has inevitably grown from the nineteenth-century custom of calling candidates for diaconate out of their congregations and incorporating them within separate communities dedicated to works of service. In effect this was to deprive candidates of the support of a congregation and to deprive congregations of an opportunity to respond as a community to the call of the Lord in their midst. An unfortunate side-effect was to isolate the deacon's *diakonia* from its social source in the church and from its sacred roots in the liturgy. The result has been that the whole of the deacon's *diakonia* has become identified with forms of social welfare to the immense loss of the values once carried by the term *diakonia* within Christian communities and indeed within their sacred scriptures.

If the church wished not to disregard those scriptural values in its corporate structures and administrative procedures, a work of considerable educational depth would need to be undertaken. To support both the congregation's understanding of its relationship to its deacons and the deacons' own sense of their being integrated into the congregation, the church needs to develop a fuller understanding of *diakonia* itself. To re-instate in the church an understanding of *diakonia* that is compatible with the Bible, and which makes additional values available once more to the diaconate, one would have to project a new vision of *diakonia*. As presently conceptualized, *diakonia* is the work of the church to meet all forms of human need. To congregations the word says little more than engagement in large programmes of social welfare.

These widespread perceptions create two problems. One arises from the fact that in the scriptures, as throughout ancient Greek, the word never carried any suggestion of welfare. To leave the impression that it did is to do violence to the real values conveyed by an important term in the scriptures and early tradition.

A second problem is then immediately upon the church. If the congregation think *diakonia* and deacons are defined by their connection with social work, they will export the idea of welfare back into scriptural passages where such an idea is going to be irrelevant and misleading. However, the church cannot leave itself open to the criticism that it does not contest public misconceptions about its scriptures. Hence the need for the church to implement educational measures of some kind to provide congregations with an understanding of *diakonia* that works in fidelity to the bible. A high sense of this responsibility was what guided John Calvin in his creation of a reformed diaconate. As noted by Elsie McKee in *Diakonia in the Classical Reformed Tradition and Today* (1989:61–62),

> For John Calvin as well as for Martin Luther, theology was the fundamental source and shaper of the teaching on *diakonia*. This was not just any theology, however; the whole intent of Calvin's work was to proclaim and teach the Word of God purely, and this was as true for the question of the diaconate as for all the other doctrines.

Ironically, the diaconate of social welfare that Calvin instituted by this process restricted its ministry to a course from which the modern review of the ancient *diakonia* seeks to divert it.

Given the nature of the tasks undertaken by deacons in major regions of the diaconal movement, an understanding of *diakonia* must be cultivated which embraces social welfare without being simply identified with it. One way to attempt this is through the idea of a sacred commission. We have seen this application at work in chapter 2. In particular we have encountered both Paul and Luke using the word *diakonia* for the purpose of designating a delegation to Jerusalem in aid of the needy. Furthermore, in both delegations we have evidence of communities accepting their corporate responsibilities to the needy and then undertaking to select and commission their agents. In addition we have distinct indications that the term *diakonia* was used in this application in order to project the conviction that the communities were carrying out a sacred task which was theirs by reason of their being a church. The task took on its quality of holiness because it was an act of holy love from one community of 'saints' to another. Establishing this ecclesial dimension of *diakonia* would be an essential task. Just as we emphasize that deacons themselves are ecclesial by virtue of the title they receive, so congregations need to acknowledge their own ecclesial identity before they can be in a position to sustain deacons in the *diakonia* which they entrust to them.

In the world of commerce, new advertising copy, new titles and new logos can do much to generate new business. In the matter of *diakonia* the situation is different. We are not suggesting a change of words but the introduction of new meaning and value to a familiar but widely-misused word. Any educational processes to improve this situation would be challenging and complex. Nevertheless, should the processes be successful, the values for community life would far outweigh inconveniences to management.

The educational process would require a shift from the idea of service to the needy to the idea of the delegation of the community's deacons and co-helpers. In reaching an understanding of this shift and of the reasons for it, each community would also be brought face to face with its corporate responsibility to acknowledge the presence in their midst of the Lord who serves. Each community would also be led to accept a corporate response 'to effect the development of the body for its upbuilding in love' (Ephesians 4:16).

In such ways deacons themselves would gain a new profile in the congregation, and their widely-cherished role as symbols of the Lord who serves would be greatly enhanced.

Martyria, diakonia, leitourgia
If misconceptions about *diakonia* have confused modern understandings of the deacon and of the deacon's connection with the congregation, the same misconceptions have contributed in certain quarters to a confused understand-

ing of the church itself. Until the idea of the church as communion – an idea represented by another ancient Greek term, *koinonia* – emerged in recent decades as the concept within which to shape a theology of church for our time, much play was made with the trilogy *martyria, diakonia, leitourgia,* these being three New Testament words for *witness, [service], liturgy.* The terms remain prominent in much theology, and especially in theology emerging from the World Council of Churches.

Within the trilogy, however, there is a problem word. This, of course, is *service,* which we have left in parentheses in the standard translation. What the trilogy is designed to say about the church is that the church must (1) proclaim the Word; (2) display the Word in works of loving service; (3) celebrate the Word in worship. Paraphrased like this the trilogy carries much meaning. The problem with the trilogy itself, however, is that the middle element is wrongly expressed when the term *diakonia* is used. The only correct Greek word would be *agapē,* love. Locked into the slogan, the term *diakonia* is stamped in the public consciousness as an expression for service to the world. Because the term is known to be a loan word from the New Testament, it carries a feigned biblical authority for an idea that the biblical term could never express.

Appropriated in this way to this trilogy and restricted in meaning to the level of loving service, the term *diakonia* is no longer available to remind congregations of the majestic notions of God's revelation of which it is the main expression in the writings of Paul or of the sacred commission to proclaim the revelation, of which it is the main expression in Luke. How do we arrive at an appreciation of 'the ministry of reconciliation' (2 Corinthians 5:18) as the peak New Testament expression of the Christian mystery when Paul's word for 'ministry' is understood as the damaged and impoverished *diakonia* of current usage? By contrast, when a congregation comes to experience that by the church's 'ministry/*diakonia* of the Spirit' (2 Corinthians 3:8) they are 'all changed from one degree of glory to another' (2 Corinthians 3:18), then they will know that the Spirit of revelation is directing them to the works of love.

The outcome of works of love is the same whether one responds to a slogan or to the direction of the Spirit, but only one of these two processes is ecclesial in the way that the New Testament was teaching the church to be. Just as 'the ministry/*diakonia* of the Spirit' is the ongoing experience of the Word of revelation in the church, and thus essentially an ecclesial experience, so is the 'minister/*diakonos*' – the deacon – an essentially ecclesial person. The deacon's title originated deep within the religious consciousness of small groups of believers towards the end of the first century and was chosen to remind the deacon and to display to the congregation that this person belonged to the church. In the solemn words and rich symbolisms of ordinations and commissionings before gatherings of believers today, the church sends deacons to be present to the church and to do what the church sees needs to be done. The works will be the works of the church.

Faith and love

Are we to limit the ecclesial dimension of the deacon to works of love? If an *ekklesia* or church lives by faith, and works by love, is one free to surmise that for deacons to be fully ecclesial persons they have a part too in the church's life of faith? Proclamation of the gospel is an ancient element in the commissioning of deacons, but is this merely the reading of the Word during the liturgy? Luther rightly dismissed that as a constitutive function of an ordained ministry. The memory we have of Lawrence of Rome might be of his gridiron and his poor, but the ancient images created for the church's memory of Lawrence present him also with the book of the gospels in his hand. This symbolizes more than the ritual proclamation. As an ecclesial person, the deacon must be close to the Word.

In writing an Afterword many years ago to the book

Diakonia: Re-interpreting the Ancient Sources I commented
on some ministerial aspects of the modern church, including the diaconate. At the time, and still today, I was struck
by reflections of the pastoral dimension of the diaconate
which T. F. Torrance included in his booklet *The Eldership
In The Reformed Church* (1984). Without going into
elements of his discussion peculiar to situations in the
Reformed Church, I would like to return to what seems to
me to be a value much overlooked in our considerations of
what might make up an ecclesial diaconate.

Torrance described the diaconate as 'an essentially
spiritual and evangelical *diakonia'*. Deacons would
possess 'a complementary ministry within the congregational life and activity of God's people'. The expression
'congregational life and activity' is, of course, comprehensive. As well as comprehending what deacons are
already providing to the church, the expression was
pointing to a neglected aspect of congregational or ecclesial life. This was the congregation's response to the
Word. To dispense the Word and Sacraments '*to* the
people', he wrote, a minister is especially ordained. He
suggested, however, that the church would benefit
greatly if this ministry were to be complemented by a
ministry of deacons to 'help the people in their reception
of the Word and in their participation in the Sacraments,
and to seek the fruit of the Gospel in the faith and life of
the community.'

Church of England Working Party 2001

Such a ministerial arrangement would present one set of
questions and problems to deacons, and different sets of
questions and problems to presbyters and pastors, synods,
councils, bishops, popes and – not least – local congregations. In every case, however, a new diaconal configuration
would require a new role description in terms of a more
wholly ecclesial diaconate. The report *For such a time as this*
produced in October 2001 by an Anglican working party
did indeed conclude with exploratory suggestions in

moving towards a new job description for 'renewed' deacons (pp. 50–60). The suggestions aimed to meet the particular circumstances of the Church of England, and were creative within that complex framework. In the light, however, of the inherently ecclesial character of the minister/*diakonos*/*deacon* which our reflections have attempted to emphasize, one would like to take further the report's own earlier ideas about the representative character of all ministry (pp. 25–28). Its understanding of 'representativeness' brings ministry into 'close relationship with the community'. This is so to such an extent that ministry is 'fundamentally relational' (p. 25). To what extent might we be invited to recognize the relational quality in the diaconate?

In our earlier reflections on how the letter to the Ephesians echoes Paul's own insistence upon a relationship between minister and believer, we too have recognized the relational character of ministry as integral to the ministry/*diakonia* of the word under examination there. The same relational quality was apparent also in the ministry/*diakonia* which Paul and his associates carried out in conveying gifts from the churches in Asia to the church in Jerusalem. In this instance the mandating churches selected their representatives, furnished them with gifts, and authorized them to affirm the far-flung Gentile churches' spiritual bonds with the mother church. Given this inbuilt relational character of ministry/*diakonia*, we have every reason to suspect that we have something further to explore in turning to reconsider practical measures for the diaconate today. In a process as intimate as ministry, then, we are going to miss something of its relational character if the measures are designed to point in one direction only, as from the minister to the church. As relational, ministry is, rather, a two-way process. Thus, as well as proceeding from minister to church, the ministry of the deacon would, in addition, ask of the congregation itself a heightened awareness of its own responsibility towards the deacon. As the report noted on

p. 25, in a citation from an earlier document, 'The responsibility of certain people to act for all is rooted in a sense of
relationship between them and the community.' The
pursuit of a real level of genuine mutuality in the *diakonia*
of the deacon would be enlivening for the congregation
and enriching for the deacon. It would also be a constant
witness to all of the vitality of the Body of Christ.

In reading, in places like internet chat groups, of
deacons' personal experiences one continually encounters
stories about deacons' individual experiences of a call. In
due course the call prompts contact with church authorities which, each in its own way, put the called persons
through interviews, psychological tests, selection panels,
and finally invite them to preliminary studies before
taking up a course over some years in deacon school or
seminary. Sometimes the individual's congregation has an
early say in approving the candidature. Often also the
candidate speaks of the challenge involved in discerning
the pastoral sector in which he or she hopes to carry out
the ministry of diaconate. Ordination and appointment
follow. The pattern would seem to owe much to pre-existing procedures for selecting candidates for the training for
the presbyterate.

Of its nature, however, deacons' ministry, varied as it
has already shown itself capable of being and full of
potential to take on other varied forms, is directed to and
indeed conditioned by local needs and circumstances.
Where the presbyterate engages itself in the catholic
dimension of Christian experience – the universal Word
and its expression in Sacrament – the diaconate has first to
authenticate itself in the life of the local congregation and
its larger community. The congregation in the first place is
where the ministerial relationship arises, and only
through fruitful mutuality there do ministerial relationships establish themselves beyond. Accordingly, it would
seem that there could hardly be a call more connatural to
the diaconate – or one more compelling – than a call from
the congregation itself.

Fruitful mutuality

In the interplay between a congregation and its deacons a new texture of mutually-acknowledged responsibilities and faithful endeavours could enrich the life of the church as a whole. The congregation would become aware of its need to know just who made up its numbers and with which qualities its members were endowed. In turn, the congregation and its deacons would target objectives within the capacities of the deacons, these being necessarily limited by the fact that most deacons would be non-stipendiary. Here we would have a mandate which is not just a prescription or a job description but mandated ministry nonetheless. And the much-bruited tag of 'go-between' would be designating something that is not merely notional but dynamic.

Neither bishop nor deacon need concern themselves about inroads into the foundational relationship created between them by ordination. Bishops would indeed have every reason to congratulate themselves on being at the heart of congregations which had become more vigorous and generous in their reception of the gospel. Bishops themselves know that for centuries their true pastoral role has been hampered – perhaps denied them in fact – by the sheer scale of their responsibilities. And the responsibilities which appear most pressing and burdensome – administrative and canonical – are largely not of a kind which the modern deacon should be called upon to share. At the same time the sheer attractiveness of a renewed pastoral life among congregations would invite closer and more personal bonds between bishop, deacons, and congregations. Bishops' roles in the selection and endorsement of new candidates would establish the relational situation in which diaconal initiatives thrive. Again, in the event of deacons needing to move on from one congregation to another, as is likely to be increasingly necessary in our mobile times, all parties would again have to be in close personal encounter in the processes of closing one relationship and establishing another. At times the other might not present itself.

Why ordain?

Innovative and stimulating as the Anglican report has shown itself to be, its line of thinking is only rarely represented in other investigatory writing. We have noted, for example, Sven-Erik Brodd's insistence on the ecclesial responsibility attaching to the deacon's *diakonia* as a consequence of ordination. As things are generally, however, with almost the entire emphasis of role descriptions lying on works of charity, many voices ask why the church needs to incorporate deacons into their role by the process of ordination. On the other hand, by requiring a role for deacons within the faith-life of the church as well as within its works of love the church would have sound reason to express the deacons' mandate through ordination. A mandate to participate in sustaining the life of faith can find expression in many forms. Some deacons already deliver homilies, but numerous other situations provide opportunities for deacons to engage themselves in the Word in ways that would not require of them the more specialized education that presbyters receive. Nor need all of these by any means be liturgical occasions like baptisms or funerals or even require public speaking. The Anglican report just mentioned surveys possibilities with a practical eye but also with sensitivity in regard to what is involved and to the impact of that upon established and developing pastoral practice. At the same time, as the writers of the report were also aware, all observers – and most members of congregations – are conscious of the failing pastoral effectiveness of parish structures today. The complex sociological patterns of life in the post-industrial world have effectively exposed the inadequacies of pastoral strategies which churches have inherited from earlier forms of society. Experimentation and research, including field research, could well reveal that a community's deacons could be effective contributors to a renewed pastoral practice.

The fact that such innovations would probably require gradual change in existing ministerial order will appear to many as a deterrent, but there could also be many potential members of congregations who would be cheered by some such prospect. The situation brings to mind a personal conviction of many years, one expressed in the conclusion of the first paper I wrote on the diaconate in Tantur, Israel, in 1977. This was that there would be no complete renewal of the diaconate until the church sees a renewal of the epis-copate. In the years when the nineteenth-century diaconate was emerging, Johann Hinrich Wichern was braver and perhaps wiser than we have managed to be. He specified that his 'brothers' should not be called deacons until condi-tions existed in the church that would allow their ecclesial character to be fully expressed through ordination.

Pathfinders

Deacons of today perhaps reflect at times on the fact that they are the first innovation in the ministerial order of the historical churches for 500 years. Deeper reflection along these lines is certainly warranted. To conclude these reflections, let us return to what Luke was doing for the church of his day – and the church he was anticipating in generations to follow – when he wrote his account of the commissioning of the Seven in Acts 6.

If we can be confident of the reading we gave earlier of Luke's story, a reading which presents the story as a theo-logical paradigm of how the church should guarantee a continuing and expanding supply of ministry (*diakonia*) of the word and eliminates any thought of deacons from Luke's intention, what values are today's deacons to look for in the account of the institution of the Seven? Although some deacons may at first feel a sense of loss or a degree of uneasi-ness at having a much-loved story seemingly taken from their hands, they ought to return to the story with new eyes.

The story unfolds in a rich setting. Luke has prepared for this story with the story of the commissioning of the Eleven by the Lord himself. This was a developing story alive with new hope and vision as the Lord pointed to the distant lands, of huge new energies and courage as the Spirit arrived, of intimacy, love and mutual dependency as the believers cohered into a closely bonded community. And this community stands in the sidelines, as it were, modelling what all future communities of believers could be as Luke's bold missionaries are carried by the word through the thronging Temple in Jerusalem, in and out of prisons and punishments, and out upon the road to Rome and beyond.

For today's deacons it is important to get the sense of Luke's vibrant scenario because it was only at a point of crisis, at a point where resources were failing, that the church took it upon itself to re-interpret the mandate which it had received from the Lord. In Luke's telling of it, that mandate had been so faithfully addressed by the Eleven that they re-instituted the original college of the Twelve to carry out the mandate. Within the framework of that picture of fidelity we can appreciate the daring of Luke at chapter 6 of Acts in presenting another scene where the Twelve re-assess the situation which their very success had brought upon the church, namely, that they were not providing complete nurture to the community itself.

At this juncture Luke presents them as doing the necessary Christian thing. They take the liberty of appearing to go beyond the Lord's own mandate by turning back to the community and seeking out its wisdom. The community itself is to find the ministerial resources that it needs for its life and health. This is consultation at its truest level. The Twelve also do a very churchly thing. They accept the wisdom of the community's choice, join with them in prayer, and by the age-old symbol of an imposition of their hands, bring the Seven under the same mandate which they had themselves received.

Can today's deacons see here images of what today's church has been attempting to do? Can today's deacons measure the appropriateness and level of success of our church's modern innovations against the old in regard to both the process and the mandate of the new diaconate? Are there avenues that deacons and their advisers are yet to explore which might lie obscured within the intriguing fabric of Luke's teaching?

Authors and works cited

Church documents

Baptism, Eucharist and Ministry, Faith and Order Paper 111 (Geneva: World Council of Churches 1982)

Deacons in the Church, Report of a Working Party set up by the Advisory Council for the Church's Ministry (Westminster: Church Information Office 1974)

Deacons in the Ministry of the Church. A Report to the House of Bishops of the General Synod of the Church of England (London: Church House Publishing 1988)

For such a time as this. A renewed diaconate in the Church of England, A report to the General Synod of the Church of England of a Working Party of the House of Bishops (London: Church House Publishing 2001)

Flannery, A., ed., *Vatican Council II. The Conciliar and Post Conciliar Documents* (Dublin: Dominican Publications 1977)

The Diaconate as Ecumenical Opportunity, The Hanover Report of the Anglican-Lutheran International Commission (London: Anglican Communion Publications 1996)

The Study of Ministry. Study Edition. Report to the 1991 Churchwide Assembly (Chicago: Evangelical Lutheran Church in America Division for Ministry 1991)

Together for Ministry. Final Report and Recommendations Task Force on the Study of Ministry 1988–1993 (Chicago: Evangelical Lutheran Church in America Board of the Division for Ministry 1993)

St Neots Deanery Synod, 'A Place for Deacons in Today's Church: a concept for a renewed diaconate. Motions regarding the diaconate from the St Neots Deanery Synod (196) to Ely Diocesan Synod and from Ely Diocesan Synod (1997) to the General Synod of the Church of England.' (Signed 20 January 1997 by John Beer, Diocesan Director of Ordinands, Richard Noble, St Neots Deanery Synod, Jeff Watson, Archdeacon of Ely.)

Books and articles

Anon., 'On the arrogance of deacons', *De iactantia Romanorum levitarum*, Corpus Scriptorum Ecclesiasticorum Latinorum 50 (1908, Johnson Reprint 1963) 193–198

Barnett, James Monroe Barnett, *The Diaconate: A Full and Equal Order*, Revised Edition (Valley Forge, PA: Trinity Press International 1995)

Barnett, James Monroe, 'Diaconate defined not by word study but by early church', *Diakoneo. Deacons and their ministry in North America* 17/5(1995)1–3

Beyer, H. W., article on *diakon-* words in Gerhard Kittel, ed., *Theological Dictionary of the New Testament*, Eng. trans., vol. 2 (Grand Rapids: Eerdmans 1964)

Bibel 2000 (Stockholm: Verbum Förlag 1999)

Bloth, Peter C., 'Zur theologischen Diakonie-Forschung', *Theologische Rundschau* 57(1992)83–95

Bloth, Peter C., 'Zur theologischen Diakonie-Forschung', *Theologische Rundschau* 66(2001)240–59

Borgegård, Gunnel and Hall, Christine, eds., *The Ministry of the Deacon, 1. Anglican–Lutheran Perspectives* (Uppsala: Nordic Ecumenical Council 1999)

Borgegård, Gunnel, Fanuelsen, Olav and Hall, Christine, eds., *The Ministry of the Deacon, 2. Ecclesiological Explorations* (Uppsala: Nordic Ecumenical Council 2000)

Brandt, Wilhelm, *Dienst und Dienen im Neuen Testament* (Gütersloh: Bertelsmann 1931)

Brodd, Sven-Erik and others, *Diakonatet i olika kyrkotraditioner*, Nordisk ekumenisk skriftserie 27 (Uppsala: Nordiska ekumeniska rådet 1995)

Brodd, Sven-Erik and others, *The Theology of Diaconia* (Uppsala: Diakonistiftelsen Samariterhemmet 1999). Eng. trans. of *Diakonins teologi* (Verbum förlag 1997)

Brodd, Sven-Erik, 'An Escalating Phenomenon: The Diaconate from an Ecumenical Perspective', in Borgegård and Hall, *The Ministry of the Deacon*, pp. 11–50

Brodd, Sven-Erik, '*Carats* and *Diakonia* as Perspectives on the Diaconate' in Borgegård, Fanuelsen and Hall (2000), pp. 23–65

Busemann, Rolf, 'Der Diakon in der frühen Kirche. Neues Testament und Kirchenväter', 34 (3/4 1999)113–31

Butler, Alban, *The Lives of the Fathers, Martyrs, and Other Principal Saints*, vol. 8 (Dublin and London: Duffy 1866)

Clarke, Andrew D., *Serve the Community of the Church. Christians as Leaders and Ministers* (Grand Rapids/Cambridge: Eerdmans 2000)

Collins, J. N., '*Diakonia* and the Diaconate' (unpublished paper 1977)[1]

Collins, J. N., *Diakonia. Re-interpreting the Ancient Sources* (New York: Oxford University Press 1990)

Collins, J. N., 'Once More on Ministry: Forcing a Turnover in the Linguistic Field', *One in Christ* 27/3(1991)234–45

Collins, J. N., 'The Mediatorial Aspect of Paul's Role as *diakonos*', *Australian Biblical Review* 40(1992)34–44

Collins, J. N., *Are All Christians Ministers?* (Sydney/Melbourne: E. J. Dwyer/David Lovell; Collegeville, MN: Liturgical Press 1992)

Collins, J. N., 'Ministry as a distinct category among charismata (1 Corinthians 12:4–7)', *Neotestamentica* 27/1(1993)79–91

Collins, J. N., 'God's Gifts to Congregations', *Worship* 68/3(1994)242–9

Collins, J. N., 'The Diakonia of Deacons. A Personal Encounter', *Diakonia Christi* 29, Sonderheft, June (1994)100–15

Collins, J. N., 'A Ministry for Tomorrow's Church', *Journal of Ecumenical Studies* 32/2(1995)159–78

Collins, J. N., 'Many Ministries. An Unresolved Ecumenical Issue' in Philip Harvey and Lynn Pryor, eds., Festschrift Lawrence D. McIntosh, *So great a cloud of witnesses. Libraries and Theologies* (Melbourne: Uniting Church Theological Hall and the Australian and New Zealand Theological Library Association 1995), pp. 220–32

Collins, J. N., 'Opening a dialogue with James Monroe Barnett on the occasion of the publication of the revised edition of *The Diaconate: A Full and Equal Order*', *Diakoneo. Deacons and their*

---

1 Some of my own writings listed here explore particular issues in more detail than the main book of 1990 did. Others, however, advance issues significantly, in particular in regard to Acts 6 (the book of 1992 and the article of 1998), the interpretation of 1 Corinthians 12:4–7 (the 1992 book again, but also articles of 1993 and 1994), and the place of women in ministry (articles of 1998, 1999, 2001). The article of 1995, 'A Ministry for Tomorrow's Church', attempts a comprehensive account of ministry in the light of the research into *diakonia*; a footnote also provides information on where to find reviews and critical comment on the two books.

ministry in North America 17/3(1995)1–4

Collins, J. N., 'Deacons considered within the nature of the church', *Diakoneo. Deacons and their ministry in North America* 18/2(1996)3–6

Collins, J. N., 'Did Luke Intend a Disservice to Women in the Martha and Mary Story', *Biblical Theology Bulletin* 28/3(1998)104–11

Collins, J. N., 'Learning about the Ministry from the Seven', *Deacon Digest* 15/3(1998)26–30

Collins, J. N., 'Does Equality of Discipleship Add Up to Church? A Critique of Feminist *Ekklesia*-logy', *New Theology Review* 12/3(1999)48–57

Collins, J. N., 'Diakoni – teoria – praxis', *Svensk kyrko tidning* 96/11 17 March: 107–11 (co-author Kjell Nordstokke)

Collins, J. N., 'Contextualizing Dorothea Reininger's Women Deacons' at http://www.womenpriests.org/called/collins3.htm

Connolly, R. H., *Didascalia Apostolorum* (Oxford: Clarendon 1929), cited according to White, *Social Origins*

Craighill, Peyton G., ed., *Diaconal Ministry, Past, Present and Future. Essays from the Philadelphia symposium, 1992* (Providence, RI: North American Association for the Diaconate 1994)

Crain, Margaret Ann and Jack L. Seymour, *A Deacon's Heart. The New United Methodist Diaconate* (Nashville: Abingdon 2001)

Danker, Frederick William, ed., *A Greek-English Lexicon of the New Testament and other Early Christian Literature*, 3rd edn., (BDAG), revised and edited by Frederick William Danker, based on Walter Bauer's *Griechisch-deutsches Wörterbuch zu den Schriften des Neuen Testaments und der frühchristlichen Literatur*, 6th edn., ed. Kurt Aland and Barbara Aland, with Viktor Reichmann, and on previous English editions by W. F. Arndt, F. W. Gingrich, and F. W. Danker (Chicago and London: University of Chicago Press 2000)

Didascalia Apostolorum, ed. R. H. Connolly (Oxford: Clarendon 1929), cited (abridged) from White, *Social Origins of Christian Architecture*, pp. 82–83

Eisen, Ute E., *Amtsträgerinnen im frühen Christentum. Epigraphische und litararische Studien* (Göttingen: Vandenhoeck and Ruprecht 1996)

Faivre, Alexandre, '"Servir": les dérives d'un idéal. D'un

ministère concret à une étape ritualisée', Haquin and Weber, *Diaconat* (1997), pp. 57–76

Farrer, A. M., 'The Ministry in the New Testament' in Kenneth E. Kirk, ed., *The Apostolic Ministry* (London: Hodder and Stoughton), pp. 113–82

FitzGerald, Kyriaki Karidoyanes, *Women Deacons in the Orthodox Church: Called to Holiness and Ministry* (Brookline, Mass.: Holy Cross Orthodox Press 1999)

Georgi, Dieter, *The Opponents of Paul in Second Corinthians*, Eng. trans. (Philadelphia: Fortress 1986; German original *Die Gegner des Paulus...* 1964)

Hall, Christine, 'Researching the Diaconate: An Anglo-Nordic Project (1997–2002)' in Borgegård and Hall, *The Ministry of the Deacon*, pp. 51–7

Hall, Christine, 'The Deacon in the Church of England' in Borgegård and Hall, *The Ministry of the Deacon*, pp. 181–247

Hall, Christine, and Hannaford, Robert, eds., *Order and Ministry* (Leominster: Gracewing 1996)

Hall, Christine, ed., *The Deacon's Ministry* (Leominster: Gracewing 1991)

Hammann, Gottfried, *L'amour retrouvé. La diaconie chrétienne et le ministère de diacre, Du christianisme primitif aux réformateurs protestants du XVIᵉ siècle* (Paris: Cerf 1994)

Hannaford, Robert, 'Foundations for an Ecclesiology of Ministry' in Hall and Hannaford, *Order and Ministry*, pp. 21–60

Hansson, Mats J., 'Diakonins teologi. Ett försök att ställa de grundläggande frågorna', *Tro & Tanke* 1999/2, pp. 11–61

Haquin, André and Weber, Philippe, *Diaconat, XXIe siècle. Actes du Colloque de Louvain-la-Neuve 13–15 septembre 1994* (Brussels: Lumen Vitae 1997)

Hünermann, Peter and others, edd., *Diakonat. Ein Amt für Frauen in der Kirche – Ein frauengerechtes Amt?* (Ostfildern: Schwaben-verlag 1997)

Käsemann, E., 'Ministry and Community in the New Testament', *Essays on New Testament Themes*, Eng. trans. (London: SCM 1964), pp. 63–94

Kasper, Walter, 'Der Diakon in ecclesiologischer Sicht angesichts der gegenwärtigen Herausforderungen in Kirche und Gesellschaft', *Diaconia Christi* 32 (3/4 1997)13–33; 'The Ministry of the Deacon', Eng. trans. of the same address to the IDC Conference on the Diaconate, Bressanone, October 1997,

Deacon Digest 15/2(March/April 1998)19–27; also http://deacon.net/Articles/Kasper–1997.htm

Keely, Avril, 'The Permanent Diaconate and the Service Model of Diaconal Ministry', *The Australasian Catholic Record* 77(2000)299–306

Kohler, Marc Edouard, *Vocation, service compris! La diaconie de l'Église* (Le Mont-sur-Lausanne: Ouverture and Geneva: Labor et Fides 1995), a translation and adaptation of *Kirche als Diakonie* (Zurich: Theologischer Verlag 1991)

Kraus, Theodore W., *The Order of Deacons: A Second Look* (Hayward, CA: Folger Graphics 1997)

Küng, Hans, *The Church*, Eng. trans. (New York: Sheed and Ward 1967)

Laghé, Birgitta, 'Diaconia – ecclesiological perspectives of diaconia and diaconate', in Brodd and others, *The Theology of Diaconia*, pp. 45–62

Legrand, Hervé, 'Le diaconat dans sa relation à la théologie de l'Église et des ministères' in Haquin and Weber, *Diaconat* (1997), pp. 13–41

Lightfoot, J. B., 'The Christian Ministry' in *Saint Paul's Epistle to the Philippians* (London: Macmillan 1891), pp. 181–269

McKee, Elsie Anne, *Diakonia in the Classical Reformed Tradition and Today* (Grand Rapids: Eerdmans 1989)

McKee, Elsie Anne, *John Calvin on the Diaconate and Liturgical Almsgiving* (Geneva: Droz 1984)

Müller, Gerhard Ludwig, *Priestertum und Diakonat. Der Empfänger des Weihesakramentes in schöpfungstheologischer und chistologischer Perspektive* (Freiburg: Johannes 2000)

Murphy-O'Connor, J., review of Collins, *Diakonia* (1990), *Revue biblique* 102/1(1995)151–3

Nordstokke, Kjell, 'The Diaconate: Ministry of Prophecy and Transformation' in Borgegård, Fanuelsen and Hall (2000), pp. 107–30

Olson, Jeannine E., *One Ministry Many Roles, Deacons and Deaconesses through the Centuries* (St Louis: Concordia 1992)

O'Meara, Thomas F., *Theology of Ministry*, Completely Revised Edition (New York/ Mahwah: Paulist Press 1999)

Plater, Ormonde, *Many Servants. An Introduction to Deacons* (Boston, Mass.: Cowley 1991)

Plater, Ormonde, 'The Collins-Kittel synthesis', *Diakoneo* 17/3(Easter 1995)5

Plater, Ormonde, 'Hanover Report: diaconal ministers and deacons', *Diakoneo* 19/3(Easter 1997)7

Ratzinger, Joseph Cardinal, 'On the Essence of the Priesthood' in *Called to Communion: Understanding the Church Today*, Eng. trans. (San Francisco: Ignatius Press 1996), 105–31. German original 1991

Reininger, Dorothea, *Diakonat der Frau in der Einen Kirche. Diskussionen, Entscheidungen und pastoral-praktische Erfahrungen in der christlichen Ökumene und ihr Beitrag zur römisch-katholischen Diskussion* (Ostfildern: Schwabenverlag 1999)

Reumann, John, 'A New Review Revising Deacons and the "Servant Church" on the Basis of Greek and Early Christian Usages', *The Patristic and Byzantine Review* 10/1–2(1991)65–70

Rogerson, Bishop Barry, address to Annual General Meeting of Diaconal Association of the Church of England, in *DACE Newsletter*, May 1997, at http:societies.anglican.org/dace/

Schäfer, Gerhard K. and Strohm, Theodor, eds., *Diakonie – biblische Grundlagen und Orientierungen*, 2nd edn. (Heidelberg: Heidelberger Verlagsanstalt 1994)

Schweizer, Eduard, *Church Order in the New Testament*, Eng. trans. (London: SCM 1961)

Torrance, T. F., *The Eldership in the Reformed Church* (Edinburgh: Handsel Press 1984)

White, L. Michael, *The Social Origins of Christian Architecture*, vol. 2 (Valley Forge, PA: Trinity Press International 1996)

White, Teresa Joan, ed., *Diakonia News* (London: 2 Tavistock Road, Westbourne Park W11 1BA)

Wood, Susan K., *Sacramental Orders* (Collegeville, MN: Liturgical Press 2000)

Zagano, Phyllis, *Holy Saturday. An Argument for the Restoration of the Female Diaconate in the Catholic Church* (New York: Crossroad 2000)

Index of names

Index of early Christian literature